PRESCRIPTIONS FOR DEATH

PRESCRIPTIONS FOR DEATH

The Drugging of the Third World

Milton Silverman

Philip R. Lee

Mia Lydecker

UNIVERSITY OF CALIFORNIA PRESS
BERKELEY • LOS ANGELES • LONDON

University of California Press
Berkeley and Los Angeles, California

University of California Press, Ltd.
London, England

© 1982 by
The Regents of the University of California

2 3 4 5 6 7 8 9

Library of Congress Cataloging in Publication Data

Silverman, Milton Morris, 1910–
    Prescriptions for death.

    Includes index.
    1. Underdeveloped areas—Drug trade—Corrupt
practices. 2. Underdeveloped areas—Pharmaceutical
policy. I. Lee, Philip R., 1924–   . Lydecker, Mia,
1926–   . III. Title.
HD9665.6.S53   338.4'76151'091724   82–1896
ISBN 0–520–04721–4   AACR2

CONTENTS

TABLES

PREFACE

While there are some who, even today, insist fanatically that modern drugs represent an unalloyed blessing for the health of the Third World, and others who proclaim that drugs have been an unmitigated disaster, it would appear that on balance, these agents have done far more good than harm. Because of the dangers inherent in any effective therapeutic compound, some use of drugs has been associated with needless injury, suffering, and death. But drug therapy has given us a degree of control over pain, crippling, disability, and early death that was unknown a century ago.

In the same way, there are some enthusiasts who proclaim that the drug industry—especially the profit-making industry—can do no right and others who are convinced that it can do no wrong. There are those who are convinced that the drug companies should be freed of all regulatory shackles. Any irresponsible company, they declare, will inevitably be controlled by the pressures of the marketplace; it will lose the confidence of patients and physicians, and its sales will suffer. The idea is terrifying. We have seen, certainly in the United States, too many examples of companies which have marketed ineffective products, dangerous or even lethal products, atrociously overpromoted products, or products that received government approval only on the basis of fraudulent evidence, and which were *not* punished in the marketplace. Even after their misdeeds were made public, they remained in business; furthermore, their annual sales, their profits, and the value of their shares on the New York Stock Exchange remained virtually unscathed. In contrast, there are those who are positive that regulation of the drug industry must be tightened by even more restrictive national or international

laws, and that no company dealing with products so important for
health and life should be permitted to make any profit. This concept,
too, we find frightening. The record of government-owned companies in
socialistic countries in developing improved drugs for the future, to control diseases which to date cannot be controlled, or even in turning out
products of acceptable quality, is scarcely reassuring.

The problem of whether or how to control drugs is of particular importance to the peoples of the Third World, living in countries described
variously as "undeveloped," "underdeveloped," "less developed," or
"developing." (We prefer the last term: it indicates at least a feeling of
optimism.) In spite of the numerous definitions that have been proposed, we find great difficulty in drawing a hard-and-fast line between
developing countries on the one hand and industrialized countries on the
other. There are clearly stages in development, with countries like
Singapore, Taiwan, and Korea occupying a middle zone between the
obviously poor countries, such as Bangladesh, Ethiopia, Mozambique,
and Tanzania, at one extreme, and Japan, the United States, and Switzerland at the other.

For a variety of reasons, the people in the developing countries appear to be at the greatest risk from the manner in which drug products
are marketed and from what can be described only as a blatant double-
standard of drug promotion:

— In the industrialized nations, because of the existence and enforce-
    ment of appropriate laws and regulations, and perhaps the social
    responsibility of the drug companies, claims of drug efficacy are
    limited to those which can be supported by convincing scientific
    evidence, and hazards are openly disclosed.

— In the Third World, because of the nonexistence or nonenforcement
    of laws and regulations, and perhaps the social irresponsibility of
    the companies, claims of product efficacy are exaggerated to an
    almost ludicrous degree and hazards—some of them life-threaten-
    ing—are minimized or not even mentioned.

Others have made similar charges. We are documenting them.

As we are noting in this book, many companies—multinational and
domestic, capitalistic and socialistic alike—have sought in many ways to
explain and defend their practices: "We are doing what the local health

officials tell us to do"; "We are breaking no laws" (in some countries, they *are* breaking the laws); "If the physicians want more information, they can write to us"; or, most commonly, "Things are different in the Third World." On analysis, it is apparent that such arguments, no matter how comforting they have been to stockholders, do not hold much water. The companies seem to pay no attention to what may be the most impelling explanation: "We make more money that way."

Associated with the existence of clinically irrational drug promotion in developing countries, and possibly associated with the success of this kind of promotion, is the traditional system of bribery and corruption. The unnerving term here is *traditional*.

For centuries, American and European merchants have sought to defend their misdeeds in Africa, Asia, and Latin America by insisting that local merchants had long been doing the same things to their own people. In many developing countries, it was pointed out, such practices as slavery, land-stealing, cruelty, and torture were well established long before the creation of colonial empires. The Europeans and the Americans simply made these practices more efficient, with perhaps a better cost-benefit ratio.

In the modern Third World, especially where drugs are concerned, the same kind of defense is an accepted procedure. "What's so bad about giving a bribe to a government official?" asks the representative of a British drug firm in India. "The Indian drug companies are doing it."

An official of a Swiss company in a West African country says, "Of course, we don't disclose all the dangers when we promote our products. But don't criticize us. The local companies don't disclose *any* of the dangers of their drugs."

But the bribery, the mislabeling, and the medically unjustified over-promotion conducted by many multinational companies cannot be ignored on the grounds that these practices are no more reprehensible than the shoddy operations of local or domestic firms. It is the multinationals—or, at least, their spokesmen in corporate headquarters—who boast of their greater respect for scientific fact, their honesty, and their superior recognition of social responsibility. There is also a difference in the order of magnitude. With their modern marketing techniques, their sophisticated methods of advertising and promotion, and their ready access to money for corruption, the multinationals can—unless appropriate steps are taken—create far more havoc, injure more victims, and kill more patients. This book attempts to examine some of these appropriate steps.

Some of these approaches may be endorsed by certain special interest groups, each of which seems to have supreme confidence in its ability to know what is best for patients. (If there is one best way, we must confess that we do not know what it is.) Some will be opposed. Some will be ignored.

It is our hope that these and other options will be evaluated not only by governmental agencies, national and international, or by the drug industry, organized medicine (as distinct from the judgment of individual physicians providing care for individual patients), or spokesmen for consumer activist groups (as distinct from consumers). In addition, we believe that the most valuable recommendations will come from the unstructured, informal, but knowledgeable and tremendously influential nonorganization known simply as the medical-scientific community. It is this community which has already had an enormous effect on such matters as the control of nuclear energy, pollution, genetic engineering, and the conduct of research on human subjects. It has yet to exert its influence in the area of drug promotion, where medicine and science have been seriously misused.

In the end, the final decisions are and must remain the responsibility of the public, whether as patients, as taxpayers, as stockholders, or as citizens. The public is not infallible. It may be swayed by emotions, prejudices, political harangue, and its own needs, or what it perceives as its needs. But it is the public which can reap the benefits and which will pay the penalties. It is entitled to have the last word.

In economics, it is held in Gresham's Law that "bad money drives out good." In the case of drugs, one might wonder if a kind of Gresham's Law could work in reverse: can decent practices drive out the indecent? We believe that there is a chance for decency to triumph.

We can conceive of few if any other investigators who have worked with the cooperation of so many knowledgeable, dedicated, and deeply concerned individuals. In the United States and Europe and in Africa, Asia, and Latin America, we have been given not only the help but also the trust of many scores of individuals—physicians, pharmacologists, pharmacists, health ministers and their staff members, medical and pharmacy educators, health economists, hospital officials, a host of consumer activists, and many scientists and physicians within the drug industry itself. In both the industrialized countries and the Third World, newspaper and television reporters have provided invaluable assistance. All of these people have shared with us their knowledge and their rich experience. They have given us their guidance, counsel, and advice— some of which we did not accept. Some of them are old friends, while others have become valued new friends, regardless of whether or not we reached agreement on every point. It is impossible for us to thank them adequately for their warm hospitality. They made us welcome in their countries. They made us welcome in their homes.

Our particular gratitude goes to the following:

— in Colombia: José Félix Patiño.

— in Costa Rica: Alfonso Trejos Willis.

— in Indonesia: Iwan Darmansjah, Eric Heyzer, Ida Bagus Oka, and Rianto Setiabudy.

— in Japan: Toru Ebihara, Hiroshi Izumi, and Etsuro Totsuka.

— in Kenya: Colin Forbes, Ingemar Gahnstedt, Katya Janovsky, James Kagia, Karuga Koinange, Dorothy Kweyu, and Christopher Wood.

— in Korea: Dal-Hyun Chi, Sang-In Kim, Sang Sup Lee, Ju Kyung Shik, and Hyunduk Shin.

— in Malaysia: Anwar Fazal, Wolfgang Howorka, Mohammed Idris, Foo Gaik Sim, and Ruth Simoons-Vermeer.

— in Mexico: Emilio Rosenstein.

— in the Netherlands: M. N. Graham Dukes.

— in Nigeria: Winifred Amene, Segun Bamgbose, Evans Chidomere, Philip O. Emafu, and Ayodele Tella.

— in the Philippines: Nelia Cortes-Maramba, Wan Fook Kee, Jesus Lamanatao, Antonio Perlas, and Arsenio Regala.

— in Singapore: J. E. Gardiner, Matthew Gwee, and Koe Khoon Poh.

— in Sri Lanka: N. D. Wilfred Lionel.

— in Sweden: Olle Hansson.

— in Taiwan: Russel Chen, Weng F. Huang, and Tsu-pei and Charlotte Hung.

— in Tanzania: Albert Henn, Martha Honey, Fatumo Mrisho, Gernard Msamanga, and Leader Stirling.

— in the United Kingdom: Sarah Bartlett, P. F. D'Arcy, Oliver and Louise Gillie, Andrew Herxheimer, Charles Medawar, Dianna Melrose, David Morley, Joan Shenton, and John and Jill Yudkin.

— in the United Nations: K. Balasubramanian.

— in Zambia: P. Gerald Moore and Wedson Mwambazi.

— in the United States: Hamilton H. Anderson, Andrew Lipton, Mark Novitch, Jack Remington, Robert Richter, and, at the University of California, San Francisco, our colleagues Larry J. Davis, Jere Goyan, Robert Smith, and, most notably because of all the years they have put up with us, Eunice Chee and Dennis Seely.

The inclusion of their names does not necessarily indicate that any of the above individuals approve or disapprove of the statements in this book.

Our thanks are extended also to officials of the U.S. Pharmaceutical Manufacturers Association, the International Federation of Pharmaceutical Manufacturers Associations, and many drug companies in the United States, the United Kingdom, Switzerland, Belgium, Mexico, Indonesia, Singapore, the Philippines, and other countries for providing us with helpful background information, much of it previously unpublished, and for describing their marketing and promotional policies and practices. We are indebted to associations of pharmaceutical manufacturers in various countries for their assistance in identifying the location of the corporate headquarters of their member companies.

Our warm gratitude also goes to leaders of the International Organization of Consumers Unions in the Netherlands and especially in Malaysia, OXFAM in Oxford, Social Audit in London, the American Association of Retired Persons in Washington, D.C., and other consumer groups who spent many days or even weeks of time in discussing their problems, programs, and policies, and in assisting us in collecting and verifying information.

We owe a particular debt to numerous industry representatives and government officials in the Third World who provided us with invaluable information and who, because of their very real fear of corporate or political punishment, asked us to protect their identities. We have kept our pledge. Their names have not been disclosed.

The many months of on-the-spot investigations during 1974, 1979, 1980, and 1981 would have been impossible without the aid of the Ford Foundation in New York, the Janss Foundation in Los Angeles, the KICADIS Foundation in Tokyo, and the Samuel Rubin Foundation in New York. They provided not only generous financial support but also their encouragement, trust, and confidence but absolutely no interference.

Once more, we must acknowledge the support of Grant Barnes of the University of California Press and his talented staff who made our work far easier than we had any right to expect, the help of Gladys C. Castor who once again did a superlative job of editing under extreme pressure, and the guidance of Jo Stewart who, after all this time—good heaven! has it really been forty years?—remains our favorite literary agent.

Finally, our affectionate thanks to Arthur Z. Cerf, M.D., and Joseph Silvestri of San Francisco for salvaging what was left of the senior author after too many months of work in Africa and Asia. And above all, our gratitude and love to Penny Shanks for keeping the home typewriters burning during our prolonged absences, and for helping to take a mountain of notes (most illegible and rumpled by too many customs inspections), tape recordings, unpublished manuscripts, minutes of meetings, reprints, foreign drug compendia and formularies, and various ill-assorted tabular data and—with unfailing dedication and good humor—turning it all into a book.

San Francisco, December 1981   Milton Silverman
                                                     Philip R. Lee
                                                     Mia Lydecker

A NOTE ABOUT THE AUTHORS

Milton Silverman, Ph.D., born in San Francisco in 1910, was trained in biochemistry and pharmacology at Stanford University and the University of California School of Medicine.

He began his career as a newspaperman on the Palo Alto *Times* and the Monterey *Peninsula Herald* in California. From 1934 to 1959, he won national recognition as the science editor of the San Francisco *Chronicle* and from 1943 to 1962 as a science writer for the *Saturday Evening Post, Collier's, Reader's Digest,* and other magazines. He is the author of *Magic in a Bottle,* a history of drug discovery, and author, co-author, or editor of twenty-one other books. He has served as a foreign correspondent in Mexico, South America, Western Europe, India, Japan, Hupeh and Szechuan provinces in China, and the South Pacific. He is a past-president of the National Association of Science Writers and a winner of the Lasker Award for distinguished medical reporting.

His own research has included studies on synthetic sugars, anesthetics, the pharmacology of alcoholic beverages, and cultural drinking patterns in Italy, Brazil, France, Sweden, and the United States. From 1959 to 1965, he was director of medical research for the Wine Advisory Board of the California State Department of Agriculture, working in many American research centers and in the Istituto di Alimentazione e Dietologia in Rome, the Institut Français d'Opinion Publique in Paris, the Karolinska Institute in Stockholm, and other centers in Moscow, Warsaw, and Prague. His technical papers have appeared in such publications as the *Journal of the American Pharmaceutical Association, California Pharmacist, Hospital Formulary, American Journal of Hos-*

pital Pharmacy, California Medicine, Annals of Internal Medicine, and *International Journal of Health Services.*

For the last fifteen years, he has been deeply involved in research on the discovery, production, promotion, pricing, prescribing, and use and misuse of prescription drugs. He has acted as a consultant to the U.S. Public Health Service, the National Institute of Mental Health, the Food and Drug Administration, and the University of Southern California School of Medicine, and, on drug insurance policies, to the Social Security Administration and the House Ways and Means Committee.

From 1966 to 1969, he served as a special assistant to Dr. Lee in Washington and again at the University of California, San Francisco, from 1969 to 1972. Since then, he has been a lecturer and research pharmacologist at UCSF's Schools of Medicine and Pharmacy, and a lecturer at the Stanford University School of Medicine.

Philip R. Lee, M.D., a member of a noted California medical family, was born in San Francisco in 1924. He was trained at Stanford University, the Massachusetts Memorial Hospital, the New York University–Bellevue Medical Center, and the Mayo Clinic.

He joined the staff of the Palo Alto Medical Clinic in 1956, working primarily as a family physician. From 1963 to 1965, he was director of health services in the Agency for International Development, and from 1965 to 1969, he was the Assistant Secretary for Health and Scientific Affairs in the U.S. Department of Health, Education, and Welfare (now Health and Human Services). He played a major role in implementing Medicare, Medicaid, and other new federal health programs.

He served as chancellor of the University of California, San Francisco, from 1969 to 1972, and has been a professor of social medicine there since 1969. In 1980–81, he was a Henry J. Kaiser Family Foundation Fellow at the Center for Advanced Study in the Behavioral Sciences at Stanford.

His own studies have involved him in such fields as health manpower, health care for the elderly, bioethics, health promotion and disease prevention, drug regulatory policies, and governmental health policies in general.

Mia Lydecker (Mia Silverman), born in The Hague, Holland, in

1926, was trained in languages and literature at the University of Utrecht, Louvain University, and the Sorbonne before coming to the United States. She began her career as a research associate with Dr. Silverman in 1962. During the past few years, she has worked with him in studying drug promotion and national drug insurance programs in Japan, Australia, New Zealand, Canada, nearly a dozen countries in Europe, and half a dozen in Latin America. Her fluency in Dutch, French, and German proved to be invaluable in many of these overseas studies.

For this present book, Ms. Lydecker and Dr. Silverman shared in undertaking the on-the-spot research in Europe, Africa, Asia, Mexico, Costa Rica, and Colombia.

During their years in Washington, Dr. Lee served as chairman and Dr. Silverman as executive secretary and staff director of the HEW Task Force on Prescription Drugs. Ms. Lydecker acted briefly as a consultant to the Task Force. The reports of this group in 1968 and 1969 led to significant changes in federal drug policies, and have had a continuing influence in many foreign countries. Their work also led to the publication in 1974 of *Pills, Profits, and Politics* by Drs. Silverman and Lee, which focused public attention on drug company policies and profits, as well as on the irrational prescribing and use of drugs. In turn, this led Dr. Silverman, with the cooperation of Ms. Lydecker and Dr. Lee, to the investigation of drug promotion by multinational drug companies in Latin America and the publication in 1976 of *The Drugging of the Americas*. In 1979, their research on drug insurance in this country and abroad resulted in the publication in 1981 of *Pills and the Public Purse*.

Since 1972, Dr. Lee has been director of what is now the Institute of Health Policy Studies, originally the Health Policy Program, at UCSF. Dr. Silverman has been a senior faculty member of the Institute, and Ms. Lydecker a staff editor and research associate.

1

THE PATIENTS

The Third World has much beauty. It has stunning mountains, rivers, jungles, grasslands, prairies, and pampas. It has fascinating cities, some old, some new. It is rich in traditions. It has diverse and ancient cultures. Its people have great pride. There is much vitality and creativity. It has music and singing and dancing, and—in some places at some times—it has happy children.

But the Third World is a hard place. For most of those who live there—and it holds nearly three-quarters of the earth's population—it means crushing poverty, overcrowded slums, squalid villages, and miserable housing. It means fever and pain and crippling, and too early death. And for most of the people most of the time, there is always hunger.

The Third World is a place of conflict. Nations war against their neighbors. Within a country, there are ancient feuds and hatreds, and tribes turn against tribes, killing or enslaving men, stealing women and cattle, destroying towns and villages and crops.

In some instances, the former colonial masters have been replaced by harsh dictatorships, at least as brutal as any of the foreign powers that once ruled the land. In others, the new governments are seeking to become democratic, socialistic, and efficient, preferably all at the same time, but generally without great success. Although colonialism is officially dead, the spirit of colonialism lives on, and great powers vie for economic and ideological control.

In the Third World nature has not yet been tamed. In some years, there are floods; in others, there are killing droughts. Biting, stinging, disease-carrying insects are almost everywhere.

The Third World has been called an invitation to disaster. If this is the case, then the invitation has been fully accepted. Sewage control and water protection in some though certainly not all countries are largely nonexistent. Only about 4 percent of the people in some areas have access to uncontaminated water.[1] Even in countries with their own international airlines, surface transportation is often slow and difficult, and sometimes dangerous. Storage facilities—especially the refrigerated storage essential for the preservation of fresh food and many medicines—are rarely available. Illiteracy is widespread; even if a package of drugs were to carry printed instructions, few people could read them. Yet, even in what seem to be the most unlikely places, there may be a television set, and the people can be exposed to television advertising. How can a country afford television when it cannot afford to buy adequate food? That is difficult to understand.

Here and there are signs of great wealth and of families who can afford luxurious homes, excellent servants, expensive cars, foreign university studies for their children, villas on the Riviera, apartments in London or New York, and safe accounts in Swiss banks. But such wealth, much of it derived from cheap plantation labor and from gold, diamonds, copper, uranium, and petroleum, does little to ease the burden of the masses.

During the last few decades, particularly since most Third World nations achieved independence, there have been notable gains in education, the development of home industries, and the provision of health care, but the needs of the people remain largely unfilled.

Especially for a child, growing up in the Third World can be an enormously dangerous affair.[2] In most of the countries, roughly one-half of all deaths strike children under the age of five. In North Yemen, it is officially estimated that one baby in six dies before reaching its first birthday, but actual surveys show that the rate may be closer to one in three; in some remote mountain areas, half will die under the age of two.[3] This is accepted. In Moslem countries, one says "It is the will of Allah."

In recent years, increasing attention has been given to the health problems of developing nations by such workers as John Fry in England, Richard Smith in Honolulu, and our own group at the University of California.[4] The staggering nature of the problems may be seen in Table 1, based mainly on data from the United Nations and the World Health Organization and presented by the World Bank.

TABLE 1. POPULATION, PRODUCTIVITY, AND HEALTH-RELATED INDICATORS IN SELECTED DEVELOPING AND INDUSTRIALIZED COUNTRIES

Country	Population (millions)	GNP per Capita	Population per MD[a]	Life Expectancy[b]	Infant Deaths[c]	Child Deaths[d]
ASIA						
Bangladesh	88.9	$ 90	8,780	49	130	19
Burma	32.9	160	5,120	54	. . .	13
India	659.2	190	3,620	52	125	15
Sri Lanka	14.5	230	6,750	66	49	3
Pakistan	79.7	260	3,760	52	. . .	15
Indonesia	142.9	370	13,640	53	120	14
Yemen Arab Republic	5.7	420	12,460	42	. . .	41
Thailand	45.5	590	8,150	62	68	6
Philippines	46.7	600	2,760	62	65	6
Malaysia	13.1	1,370	8,730	68	32	2
Korea	37.8	1,480	1,990	63	37	5
Taiwan	17.3	1,870	1,500	e	11	1
Hong Kong	5.0	3,760	1,180	76	12	f
Singapore	2.4	3,830	1,250	71	13	1
AFRICA						
Ethiopia	30.9	130	75,320	40	. . .	36
Mozambique	10.2	250	33,980	47	. . .	25
Tanzania	18.0	260	17,550	52	. . .	18
Zaire	27.5	260	15,530	47	. . .	25
Kenya	15.3	380	11,630	55	91	15
Ghana	11.3	400	9,920	49	. . .	22
Zambia	5.6	500	10,190	49	. . .	22
Nigeria	82.6	670	15,740	49	. . .	22
LATIN AMERICA						
Nicaragua	2.6	660	1,670	56	. . .	16
El Salvador	4.4	670	3,600	63	60	8
Peru	17.1	730	1,550	58	86	14
Colombia	26.1	1,010	1,970	63	65	8
Guatemala	6.8	1,020	2,490	59	. . .	13
Ecuador	8.1	1,050	1,620	61	66	10
Mexico	65.5	1,640	1,820	66	60	5
Chile	10.9	1,690	1,620	67	55	6

TABLE 1.   continued

Country	Population (millions)	GNP per Capita	Population per MD[a]	Life Expectancy[b]	Infant Deaths[c]	Child Deaths[d]
Brazil	116.5	1,780	1,700	63	92	8
Costa Rica	2.2	1,820	1,390	70	28	3
Uruguay	2.9	2,100	540	71	34	3
Argentina	27.3	2,230	530	70	. . .	3
INDUSTRIALIZED NATIONS						
Italy	56.8	5,250	490	73	18	1
United Kingdom	55.9	6,320	750	73	14	1
Austria	7.5	8,630	430	72	15	1
Japan	115.7	8,810	850	76	9	f
Canada	23.7	9,640	560	74	12	1
France	53.4	9,950	610	74	11	1
Netherlands	14.0	10,230	580	75	10	f
United States	223.6	10,630	570	74	14	1
West Germany	61.2	11,730	490	73	16	1
Sweden	8.3	11,930	560	76	8	f
Switzerland	6.5	13,920	510	75	10	f

Sources: *World Development Report 1981* (Washington, D.C.: World Bank, August 1981); for Taiwan, Taipei Department of Health, 1981.
Note: Figures shown are for 1979 or latest available data. Countries listed in each group are in order of Gross National Product (GNP), which may serve as an indication of relative poverty or wealth.
[a] Population per physician with M.D. or comparable degree.
[b] Life expectancy at birth.
[c] Infant deaths (0–1 year) per 1,000 live births.
[d] Child deaths (1–4 years) per 1,000 children in population.
[e] 69 for males, 74 for females.
[f] Less than 0.5.

Life expectancy at birth in the Third World has improved substantially in the last two or three decades. For industrialized nations in the mid-1970s, the average was about seventy-one years. For less developed countries, it was fifty-three years. But for the least developed nations, it was about forty years, a figure that corresponds roughly to that for Western Europe and the United States in the year 1850.

Infant mortality rates have been dramatically reduced in the past thirty or forty years, but they are still shockingly high in Africa, Asia, and Latin America. Rates in the mid-1970s were estimated to be less than 20 deaths per 1,000 live births in North America, Northern and Western Europe, and Japan. But in parts of West Africa the rate may be as high as 178 per 1,000 live births. These figures may be underestimations, for rates as high as 300 to 400 per 1,000 have been unofficially reported for some developing countries in some years.

Most of the important killing diseases that plague the Third World are not mysterious tropical ailments. Their nature is reasonably well understood. Some are transmitted by contaminated water or food: dysentery, typhoid fever, cholera, and polio. Some, like malaria, are carried by mosquitoes or other insects. Tuberculosis, whooping cough, and measles are spread through the air by droplet infection. Most of these are made worse, and more surely killing, by underlying malnutrition and starvation.

"Physicians in industrialized countries are unaware of health problems as they exist in the Third World," says Harvard-trained James Kagia of the University of Nairobi in Kenya. "In the United States or Europe, a doctor can treat a patient for his tuberculosis or his hypertension, or his pneumonia. In Africa, you may have to treat the patient for any one of these conditions, or all three of them together, *plus* his malaria, *plus* his dysentery, *plus* his parasitic infestation, plus God knows what else, and *especially* plus his malnutrition."[5]

This is particularly sad because practically all of these killers can be controlled. Some can be effectively limited or actually cured by drugs now readily available in developed parts of the world. Some can be virtually wiped out by sewage control, simple sanitation, the protection of water supplies, and insect control. Some can be prevented by vaccination. The problem of malnutrition can obviously be solved by the provision of adequate food, especially protein food. The tragedy lies in the fact that what can and should be done is not being done adequately.

The case of measles is noteworthy. In Africa, for example, it is considered to be one of the most dangerous of all infections.[6] In the United States and Europe, it is routinely prevented by the administration of measles vaccine; this vaccine, however, must be kept refrigerated at all times until it is injected. It has been used in Africa, but sometimes with no effect and sometimes with deadly results.

Too often, a shipment of vaccine may be held up because a truck is not available or the roads are impassable. Too often a shipment may be held for days or weeks in a warehouse without refrigeration because of incredible customs red tape, or of equally incredible bureaucratic inefficiency or bungling, and the failure to recognize that the vaccines must be handled as urgent, high-priority cargo.[7]

If there is such a delay, or a break in what is called the "cold chain," the vaccine may lose some or all of its potency. Worse, it may become harmful.

"Here in Africa," says a pediatrician, "about 20 percent of the children are vaccinated against measles. But in some places, vaccination can mean death. In some rural areas, the vaccine has produced serious side effects in nearly half of the children. Perhaps 10 percent of the vaccinated children died from these effects."[8]

But even if the vaccine were kept properly chilled, it might nevertheless be without value. If the children are malnourished, their bodies cannot develop immunity.

For those who survive the first few years of life, their prospects remain grim. In some developing countries, a third or more will be chronically malnourished or undernourished—"starved" may be too harsh a term—for their entire lifetime.[9] Perhaps 90 percent or more will acquire a parasitic infestation.[10] They will suffer from bouts of malaria or diarrheal disease, possibly four or five times each year, and often be too ill and weak to earn a living or cope with household duties. Even in an urban area like Kingston, in Jamaica, diarrheal diseases account for 37 percent of all childhood deaths.[11]

Perhaps there would be less anguish in the Third World if its inhabitants were unaware of the medical marvels available in more fortunate nations. But they *are* aware that these marvels do exist elsewhere. Halfdan Mahler, the Director-General of the World Health Organization, told a reporter from the British Broadcasting Corporation of an African village where the people demanded a new supply of chloroquine tablets for their malaria.

"In that particular village where I was," he said, "they had not seen these tablets for six months. And for that reason, out of anger, they killed the first governmental official who came to visit them."[12]

European health workers have described the desperate efforts that the people will make to obtain medicines for themselves and especially for their sick children.

"They're sick, they're frightened, they think they may die and leave their children without anyone to care for them," said a British nurse working in Bangladesh. "They are extremely vulnerable. If the doctor says you must take this, and this, and this, they will take it faithfully. They will spend their last pennies buying, for example, some vitamin preparation."[13]

She told of a gardener whose child had developed a middle-ear infection. "He brought us what the doctor had written out for him. That included three antibiotics—not one, but three!—and three vitamin preparations. Now, that was going to cost him several hundred *taka*—the average wage in Bangladesh now is eight *taka* a day—and he was going to find it, he was going to borrow it, he was going to steal it—I don't know, but he would, because his child was sick."

The Third World is indeed a hard place.

The health care systems of developing countries appear as if they were deliberately designed to keep that care as far as possible from most of the people who need it. In each country, virtually all of the hospital facilities, all of the well-equipped clinics, all of the x-ray and laboratory facilities, and most of the best-trained physicians, nurses, dentists, and pharmacists have been concentrated in two or three major cities. This arrangement was the comfortable one for the British, the French, the Spanish, the Portuguese, the Germans, the Dutch, and the Belgians who ruled the countries in colonial times. (Little credit or blame can be given to the Americans, who by then were largely out of the colony business.) The Europeans had easy access to the best care. But the system now makes health care easily available to only a small proportion— perhaps 10 or 20 percent—of the nation's population who live in the big cities. It is not so good for the 80 or 90 percent who live elsewhere, often in remote districts.

It is much as if all the health facilities were swept up from the rest of America and set down in the District of Columbia, especially if the roads in the United States were not very good, or if all the health facilities in Europe were concentrated in Belgium, in the vicinity of the Common Market headquarters.

In the Latin American countries, most of which achieved nominal independence far earlier, the concentration of medical centers seems to have been dictated not so much by the convenience of foreign rulers as by an equally simple and perhaps more equitable rule: big medical centers in big cities, smaller centers in smaller communities.

Today, in a relatively compact island country like Sri Lanka (formerly Ceylon), distances are not forbidding, and it is estimated that about 85 percent of patients can receive their care from a physician.[14] In Singapore, which may or may not be considered a member of the Third World, physician services are reasonably close at hand for almost everyone. But in nations like Kenya, Tanzania, Brazil, Pakistan, Bangladesh, and parts of India, experts say that only 5 to 20 percent of the people are treated by physicians.[15] In much of the Third World, skilled health professionals are few, travel is tortuous, and it may take many hours or days to reach a hospital.

In some parts of the Third World, care may be provided in small regional hospitals, often poorly staffed and poorly equipped. Most patients are treated in village health centers or dispensaries, usually by dedicated but overworked village nurses or physician aides or assistants who may have been given only a year or two of training.

"But in this part of the world," says a health expert in Kenya, "the most common problems are malaria, pneumonia, and dysentery. It really doesn't take five years of medical school training to tell them apart."[16]

In some remote areas, somewhat better care may be obtained in what are called mission or Christian hospitals, supported by American and European organizations. Although a physician may be at hand, he too is usually overworked. An American visitor described the hospital in a Cameroon village in these words:

> With its 100 beds the mission hospital in Nguti has only one general practitioner, a young Nigerian trained in Italy, and a nurse/technician staff of 11 Spanish Sisters and Brothers of the Order of St. John of God. The physician works six full days and is on call every Sunday. He has full responsibility for all medical and surgical care. His annual vacations leave the hospital without a replacement. In his absence the nurses provide services whose scope is defined by their courage to respond to patients' needs.

The American physician, William Minkowski, now with the Los Angeles County Department of Health Services, worked at the Nguti hospital and discovered that, even though English was supposed to be the national language of the country, there were certain problems in communications through what is termed bush-country pidgin English.

At the St. John of God Hospital, I had to lean heavily on the interpretive skills of the Sisters. . . . On occasion, a patient's answers were conveyed to me rather colorfully. For example, two common clinical symptoms in rural African males are diarrhea and impotence. My accompanying Sister-nurse, frocked from head to toe in the traditional garb of her Order, would receive the question about bowel habits from me. Her face beatifically innocent, she would ask the patient, "You no de shit fine?" Or, from the same radiant countenance, in response to my question about sexual function, emerged her direct inquiry: "Your ting, it no wake up so fine?"[17]

Those living away from the cities—which means most people—will rarely go to a pharmacy, since pharmacies do not abound there. Instead, they may visit a local general store, describe their clinical problem and symptoms, and ask the storekeeper for some particular product recommended by a friend or advertised on the radio, or for a suitable medication of his own choosing. Or they may go to a local bus stop and patronize a street vendor, who will count out a few tablets or capsules taken from an already opened, unlabeled, dust-covered container—possibly crawling with flies—whose contents may well be difficult or impossible to identify, contaminated, adulterated, overage and spoiled, and with a potency somewhere between useless and lethal. Such practices in developed countries are generally illegal and nonexistent. In the Third World, they are merely illegal.

In some communities, either urban or rural, and whether or not modern "orthodox" or "Western" medicine is at hand, patients will turn to what are known as "traditional" healers. These practitioners use various herbs and animal extracts. The treatment may include prayers, incantations, songs, incense burning, and ritual dances. Gods must be propitiated, devils exorcized, and bodies cleansed. The ingredients of the products may be highly complex, almost defying analysis. In some instances, chemists have found that the traditional drugs may be laced with steroid hormones like prednisone or antiarthritis agents like phenylbutazone.[18]

The budgets for all health care in the developing countries are pitifully small, and most of the available funds are earmarked for *curing* rather than preventing disease, even though prevention in the long run would be vastly more cost-effective and humane. This inordinate emphasis on curing, government leaders insist, comes from the fact that the people demand cures. The people in the poor countries—like many in industrialized nations—appear to be convinced that there *must* be a curative pill for every ill, and they will spend their last rupee or peso or quetzal to buy the vitamin, the hormone, or the pain-killer that will restore themselves or their children to health.[19] To help their babies grow, they will sacrifice their limited funds to buy an infant-feeding formula that, without clean water and proper sterilization, can kill their babies.

Much of this irrational and often emotional demand has stemmed from the enormous promotion and advertising campaigns, particularly for over-the-counter products, mounted by the drug industry and the food companies—advertising in newspapers, in magazines, on billboards, and on television and radio. Decent health care may not penetrate to every village, but radio advertising can.

As a result of all these pressures on the public, along with more malign influences focused on some physicians and government officials, a relatively huge portion of the limited funds available for health care is used for the purchase of drugs. Whereas drug costs for government health programs represent only about 8 to 10 percent of the health budget in the United States, Great Britain, and similar countries, they amount to roughly 22 percent in Tanzania, 24 percent in Burma, 26 percent in Zambia, 44 percent in Nepal, and more than 60 percent in Bangladesh.[20]

Even though these percentage figures seem high, they involve relatively small amounts of money. Thus, whereas per capita drug expenditures are approximately $73 per year for out-of-hospital drugs in the United States ($47 for prescription drugs and $26 for over-the-counter products), they amount to only $1.20 in Nigeria, $0.75 in India, and $0.58 in Sri Lanka.[21]

Concealed in such numbers are the costs of what would seem to be unbelievably irrational drug purchases. For example, as John Yudkin has noted, most arthritis patients can be helped by aspirin. A few who are not aided by aspirin can be relieved by a newer anti-inflammatory agent such as ibuprofen, which costs twenty-five times as much. But if one arthritis patient in a poor country gets ibuprofen, then twenty-four patients may not be able to obtain even aspirin.[22]

If one Third World victim of insomnia is given pentobarbital (Nembutal) under a government program instead of the less costly chloral hydrate, then ten patients may not be able to get any sleeping medicine because of inadequate funds. If one patient is given Hoechst's injectable tetracycline instead of the oral form, then thirty patients will not be able to obtain any tetracycline. If one patient with hookworm is given pyrantel (Combantrin) rather than the low-cost and probably more effective tetrachlorethylene, then more than fifty patients cannot get the inexpensive preparation. And if one patient is given a course of treatment with cloxacillin even though his infection is susceptible to penicillin, then more than seventy patients will be unable to get any antibiotic.[23]

And if a starving baby in a poor family is given a costly vitamin and mineral supplement like Glaxo's Calci-Ostelin B12, the family will be even poorer and the baby will still starve.

As illogical as it may seem, although the bulk of unquestionably useful drugs are needed in the towns and villages, where most patients are treated, the greatest amount of the drugs and especially the most expensive of them are sent to the big-city hospitals for the benefit of the relatively few. This has often resulted in grave shortages.

"Many outlying clinics and dispensaries receive their allotments of drugs on the first day of each month," says a physician working in Kenya, "but they run out at the end of two weeks. The same thing happens at some of the smaller hospitals."[24] Yudkin has stated, "In some rural dispensaries in East Africa, all drugs are out of stock for half the year."[25]

The same kind of thing can happen even in some of the biggest and best of the teaching hospitals. A Kenya newspaper carried this report late in 1980: "Patients undergoing minor but painful surgery for repair of injuries at Kenyatta National Hospital in Nairobi are unable to get pain-killing drugs at the hospital. Instead, their relatives are given a prescription and told to get it filled at a private pharmacy—but unfortunately, they had no funds to buy them."[26]

Much of the trouble stems from the fact that the developing nations as a whole have approximately three-fourths of the world's people, but have access to only one-fifth of the world's supply of drugs.[27] Conceivably, this problem will be solved eventually with money—money enabling the Third World to purchase the drugs it needs, and to build and operate the sewage-control systems, the water-purification plants, the insect-control programs, and whatever else is required to prevent those diseases that can be prevented.

But there is yet another problem of almost equal importance. This one concerns the way in which drugs are sold and used, and the honesty and reliability of drug-industry promotion and advertising to physicians, to pharmacists, and to the public. This problem cannot be simply solved by throwing money at it.

2

THE DRUGS

The appropriate drug, properly prescribed and properly used, may mean the difference between comfort and pain, crippling, and disability; it may mean the difference between life and death.

Much—and perhaps everything—depends on whether the product is described in the labeling and promotion so that the physician can order the right drug for the right patient, in the right amounts and at the right time, and so that he can give each patient the proper instructions for use.

Unfortunately, and sometimes tragically, the physician may be given no information or the wrong information. The necessary information may not be easily available; the prescriber may be told, for example: "See company literature." Such advice is essentially useless for an overworked physician trying to cope with hordes of patients in a crowded big-city health center, or for a physician aide struggling against the odds to provide decent care in a remote village clinic. The information may be available but ignored or misunderstood; it may be inaccurate, out-of-date, incomplete, or biased; or the prescriber—big-city physician or village health aide—may be swayed by patient pressure, peer pressure, or the intensive campaign of the drug industry.[1]

Moreover, if the labeling instructions to physicians are defective, it may be impossible to provide vital instructions to patients. If, for instance, a patient is given a bottle of tetracycline capsules and not warned against the simultaneous consumption of such calcium-containing materials as milk, cheese, and other dairy products and widely used antacids, the antibiotic will not be absorbed adequately into the body and an infection can rage unchecked.

13

During the last few years, investigators have begun to examine the reliability of prescription drug labeling and promotion, especially comparing what drug companies tell physicians in industrialized nations and what they say in the developing countries of the Third World. Among the earliest studies in this highly sensitive field were those of Robert Ledogar in 1975,[2] the documented report on the behavior of multinational companies in Latin America in 1976,[3] and the 1980 disclosure on the situation in Malaysia and Singapore by Wolfgang Howorka of the Penang, Malaysia, regional office of the International Organization of Consumers Unions.[4] Other workers have paid particular attention to drug promotion in Sri Lanka and India,[5] and in Tanzania,[6] and to the promotional activities of British pharmaceutical companies.[7] (See also Haslemere[8] and Heller.[9])

The present investigation broadens the research to cover drug company performance in the United States and Great Britain and in a number of countries in Africa, Asia, and Latin America: Ethiopia, Ghana, Kenya, Nigeria, the Sudan, Tanzania, Uganda, Zaire, Zambia, and other countries in Central Africa; Indonesia; Malaysia and Singapore; the Philippines; and the Central American countries of Costa Rica, the Dominican Republic, El Salvador, Guatemala, Honduras, Nicaragua, and Panama. Attention has likewise been devoted to drug promotional developments in industrialized or rapidly industrializing nations like Taiwan, Korea, and Japan, and the crown colony of Hong Kong.

SOURCES OF DATA

Widely used compendia of prescribing information have been examined to show the way in which drug companies describe the recommended uses of their products and disclose the major dangers. These include *Physicians' Desk Reference*, or *PDR*,[10] in the United States; *MIMS*[11] or *MIMS UK* (originally standing for *Monthly Index of Medical Specialties*) in the United Kingdom; *MIMS Africa*[12] for the countries in East, Central, and West Africa; *IIMS*[13] for Indonesia; *DIMS*[14] for Malaysia and Singapore; and *PIMS*[15] for the Philippines. In Latin America, various publications known to physicians as *PLMs*, for *Para Los Medicos*, are distributed annually in Mexico, in Central America, and in Colombia and Ecuador. As illustrative of the promotion and labeling information furnished to Latin American physicians, we have elected to use the volume for Central America, *Diccionario de Especialidades Farmacéuti-cas, Edición C.A.D.,*[16] or *PLM CAD.*

For our purposes, we have used the 1979 edition of *PLM CAD,* which was the one commonly consulted by practitioners during the year 1980. In all other cases, 1980 editions were used.

Other drug reference books are published annually or more fre-quently for some of these countries, but they are generally far less comprehensive and do not incorporate many products marketed by mul-tinational companies.

PDR is cited here, not because the statements it contains—which gen-erally reflect the attitudes of the Food and Drug Administration (FDA) and its expert consultants—are necessarily scientifically valid, endorsed by each drug manufacturer, or accepted by all physicians, or even by all expert physicians. Rather, the *PDR* descriptions are based on material that has been formally approved by an official government agency, they are at least tolerable to the drug manufacturers, and the volume is dis-tributed to all practicing physicians in the United States and frequently consulted by them.[17] Under existing laws, the statements approved by FDA for each drug must form the basis for all package inserts, medical journal advertising, and other forms of labeling and promotion.

The listings in *PDR,* the *MIMS* publications, and the *PLMs* must be considered as drug promotion or advertising, paid for by the drug com-panies that elect to list their products. *In no country is any company, domestic or multinational, legally obliged to include its products.*

In the United States, Great Britain, and the Third World countries, the publishers apparently take no responsibility for the statements the publications include. "We do not challenge the claims the companies make," says one of them. "We do not require them to disclose hazards. We simply print what the pharmaceutical firms give us to print."

This explanation has recently been challenged. In his *Drug Disinfor-mation,* analyzing the promotion and labeling of identical products list-ed in the British *MIMS* and its Irish counterpart *MIMS Ireland*—both published by the same firm—Charles Medawar says he was told by some drug companies that they do not have complete control over what is published.

"The editor of MIMS, Dr. Colin Duncan," one company spokesman wrote, "insists on having, getting and utilizing complete editorial free-dom in deciding on the contents of MIMS. This may lead to absolute disagreement with a company's view or request and even differences with Data Sheets. Thus, individual companies are quite unable to control the entries in MIMS."[18]

In his study, Medawar received less than full cooperation from the *MIMS* publisher, which declined to give or even sell copies to him on the grounds that he was not a physician or other health professional. Accordingly, Medawar was required to consult copies available in the London public library.

In the developing countries, what the advertisers "give us to print" is not significantly determined by governmental decision, as is the case in the United States. The statements are based primarily on the individual conscience, social responsibility, and business standards of each company. As will be noted below, there may be striking differences in the policies of different companies marketing the same product in the same country. There may be differences in the policies of the same company in different countries.

"There are times," a Swiss company official told us, "when we have difficulty in explaining such differences to outsiders. We sometimes have trouble in explaining them to ourselves."

In this examination of the reliability of drug promotion and labeling and the availability of this kind of information, we have surveyed the published guidelines as presented to physicians and pharmacists on some 510 drug products, brand-name or generic, marketed by more than 150 companies. Some of the firms are "domestic," operating in only one country or one region, while others are multinational, operating in many nations, industrialized or developing. Some firms are based in capitalistic nations, while others are based in communist-bloc countries.

The products chosen for study represent six major categories: antibiotics, antidiarrheals, drugs to control pain and fever, tissue-building hormones, "tonics," and oral contraceptives. The combinations classified as "tonics" are included if only to suggest the ingenuity of those who concoct drug products.

Previously, we have reported on the promotion in Latin America of such drug products as major tranquilizers, antidepressive agents, antiepilepsy drugs, cortisone-like hormones, and antiarthritis drugs.[19]

In general, each product included here meets these criteria: (1) it is a valuable drug—except perhaps for some of the tonics—and in most

cases one that is widely used; (2) it has well-established clinical usefulness and known hazards; and (3) it is usually marketed in a solid form,
that is, a tablet or a capsule, rather than as an injectable form to be
administered by a physician, nurse, or physician assistant.

Even in the few though important drug groups considered here, no
attempt has been made to include *all* products within the group. Any
such effort would have resulted only in the production of a gargantuan
encyclopedia, and taken more lifetimes than we have available.

The law in industrialized countries often stipulates what the manufacturer must say about each product and what it may not say. In the
United States, the law requires that indications or claims of efficacy be
limited to those that can be supported by what FDA considers to be
substantial scientific evidence. Claims based essentially on endorsements
("Before taking the medicine, I could lift my arm only *so* high"), wide
popularity among physicians ("I prescribe it every week"), and many
years of use—the "test of time" argument—are no longer acceptable.
Warnings, precautions, and contraindications must be given in detail.
Potential adverse reactions, ranging from mild to lethal, must be fully
disclosed.

It is the official policy of FDA, and was presumably the intent of the
Congress that enacted the legislation, that such regulations shall not
control an individual physician in making his prescribing judgments. If,
for example, an American physician decides to treat a patient suffering
from a mild skin rash with a highly potent drug approved for use only
in the treatment of inoperable cancer, his sanity must be questioned, but
he is probably breaking no FDA rule. His former professors in medical
school may view his behavior with alarm, but he is no longer in their
power. His colleagues may look upon his prescribing habits with displeasure; the chances are, however, that he will not be summoned before
them to explain—unless his erratic prescribing occurs too frequently. Of
course, if the patient is seriously injured or dies as a result, there may
be a malodorous suit for malpractice.

Physicians have generally similar freedom of prescribing in most developing nations. In Tanzania, for example, or in Sri Lanka, Bangladesh, or Malaysia, prescribers may safely ignore the advice of drug regulatory authorities. (We remain fascinated to observe that medical men
who pay not the least attention to the prescribing guidelines of drug
regulatory agencies are, in the United States and many other countries,

among those who most vigorously denounce these guidelines as intolerable governmental interference in medical practice.)

Notwithstanding the legal right of physicians to go against the prescribing recommendations for each drug product, and to pay no heed to any warnings that might be disclosed by the manufacturers, it is apparent that this published material is important. Most physicians seem to agree, for they consult such material regularly, and the copies of the published guides in their offices—especially in Third World countries—are usually dog-eared from frequent use. Most manufacturers obviously hold similar views, since they pay substantial sums each year to disseminate their promotional information.

For the clinical background sections in this chapter, there are many excellent authorities that could be used as source material. For simplicity, we have elected to cite primarily three highly and internationally respected publications: Goodman and Gilman, *The Pharmacological Basis of Therapeutics*,[20] and the American Medical Association's *AMA Drug Evaluations*,[21] in the United States, and *Martindale: The Extra Pharmacopoeia*,[22] in Great Britain. These three do not always support the statements found in *PDR*, the *MIMS* books, and the *PLMs*. They do not always agree with each other. They change from time to time as the state of knowledge changes. Together, they seem to say to prescribing physicians:

> This, at the time of publication, is the best advice to be drawn from the best scientific research now available. Ignore it at your peril—or the peril of your patients.

Throughout this chapter, it is important to note that a number of European firms are represented by subsidiaries which operate in the United States and which are not covered in this study. For example, Ciba Pharmaceutical Company and Geigy Pharmaceuticals in Summit, New Jersey, are divisions of Ciba-Geigy in Switzerland, and Roche Laboratories in Nutley, New Jersey, is part of another Swiss firm, Hoffmann-La Roche. None of the three United States–based companies, however, is engaged in the marketing of its products outside of the United States, and accordingly, its labeling and other practices are not considered here. Such subsidiaries cannot be held accountable for the policies of their parent companies.

It should also be noted that, regardless of the apparent similarities in names, there is no relation between Merck Sharp & Dohme in the United States and E. Merck in West Germany, nor between Schering Corporation (part of Schering-Plough) in the United States and Schering AG in West Germany.

ANTIBIOTICS

Since the introduction of the antibiotics, beginning spectacularly with penicillin in the mid-1940s, few other groups of drugs have been more effectively and more widely used. They have given physicians the means to control many of the dreaded bacterial infections of the past: among them bubonic plague, typhoid fever, typhus fever, cholera, pneumonia, meningitis, syphilis, and the life-threatening forms of staphylococcal and streptococcal disease. In the United States, antibiotics now account for nearly 20 percent of all prescriptions. In some Third World countries, they account for more than 45 percent.[23]

At the same time, they have been among the most widely mispromoted, misprescribed, and misused of all prescription drugs. They have been administered irrationally: the wrong drug for the wrong patient, in the wrong amounts or at the wrong time, or when no drug was required in the first place. Patients have been needlessly injured or killed. Scarce funds have been wasted, as when antibiotics have been administered for such diseases as the common cold or influenza, in which they are worthless. In spite of prolonged educational efforts, many patients—and even some physicians—have failed to learn that no antibiotic can be accepted as harmless, that any antibiotic powerful enough to injure or destroy bacteria can also injure or destroy human beings. Too often, especially in elective surgery, antibiotics are given routinely to prevent an infection in what has been described as a "pharmaceutical version of propitiating the gods." Potentially dangerous antibiotics have been prescribed when safer and equally effective alternatives are available. Costly agents have been ordered when less-expensive products could be expected to yield the same clinical results.

In addition, this needlessly excessive prescribing of antibiotics has led to the appearance of resistant bacterial strains that may sweep through an entire hospital ward, an entire hospital, or an entire province or nation. The rise of these resistant strains is not a trivial matter: it has been blamed for the needless deaths of thousands or tens of thousands of deaths a year.[24]

This situation continues to cause consternation among medical and pharmacy leaders and governmental health authorities. Much of the responsibility clearly lies on the drug companies that promote their products and on the physicians who prescribe them unwisely; equally clearly, some lies on the patients who request or even demand an antibiotic when none is justified.

Chloramphenicol

Discovered in a mould found in Venezuela in 1947, used that same year in crude form against an epidemic of typhus fever in Bolivia with dramatic results, and isolated in pure crystalline form in 1948, chloramphenicol was marketed first by Parke-Davis under the brand name of Chloromycetin. It is relatively inexpensive to produce synthetically, quickly effective when taken by mouth,* able to withstand prolonged storage, and highly effective against a wide assortment of infectious organisms. It is that last characteristic which, in a way, is responsible for much of the problem with chloramphenicol. Since it is useful in many diseases, it has been used in many diseases. And since 1950, it has been evident that this drug can produce serious and even lethal side effects.

Clinical Background. Unquestionably, medical experts agree, chloramphenicol has great value in treating certain "life-threatening overwhelming" infections caused by susceptible organisms. It remains the drug of first choice against typhoid fever and one of the best to use against *Hemophilus influenzae,* Rocky Mountain spotted fever (which occurs mainly in many areas besides the Rocky Mountains), and with other infections, including brain abscess, which may not be readily controlled with less toxic drugs.[25]

Unfortunately, the use of chloramphenicol may be associated with the development of a form of aplastic anemia, a kind of blood dyscrasia marked by reduced production of red blood cells, which is severe, often irreversible, and frequently fatal. Usually this adverse reaction occurs

---

* Products for external use only are not considered here.

after a latent period of weeks or months. It may follow prolonged therapy, or it may come after only a single treatment. There is still no way to predict which patient will develop aplastic anemia; among those who develop this condition, the death rate may be 40 percent or more.

Aplastic anemia induced by chloramphenicol is relatively rare. It may be an acceptable risk in the case of patients who, without treatment, would almost certainly die. But it is not acceptable in the treatment of patients with a cold, a case of "flu," or a sore throat.

There are other risks associated with chloramphenicol. One is the occurrence of the so-called grey syndrome, which is marked by vomiting, abdominal distension, ashen color, a fall in body temperature, irregular breathing, and shock, generally followed by death in a few hours or days. It has been reported primarily in premature and other newborn infants that were given large doses of the drug.

For such reasons, infectious-disease experts are in strong agreement that chloramphenicol should not be used for minor infections and never for prophylaxis. It should not be used in diseases that can be readily, safely, and effectively treated with such safer agents as penicillin and tetracycline. Repeated courses should be avoided if at all possible. Patients must be followed carefully by a physician. Some authorities urge that any patient on chloramphenicol treatment should have a blood count every forty-eight hours.[26]

Promotion. As is shown in Table 2, chloramphenicol products marketed in the United States and the United Kingdom are labeled in accordance with such modern scientific knowledge. The indications for use are limited and carefully spelled out. Warnings, contraindications, precautions, and major potential adverse reactions are presented clearly.

In *PDR,* physicians are reminded that serious and even fatal blood damage may occur after the administration of Parke-Davis's Chloromycetin and that this has occurred after both short-term and prolonged therapy. It is essential that adequate blood studies be made during treatment with the drug so that the treatment can be halted immediately at the first appearance of blood damage, a recommendation that would be totally unrealistic in many parts of the world. Italic type is used in *PDR* to emphasize the warning: *It must not be used in the treatment of trivial infections or where it is not indicated, as in colds, influenza, infections of the throat, or as a prophylactic agent to prevent bacterial infections.*

TABLE 2

CHLORAMPHENICOL

Products: Indications and Warnings

	WARNINGS						INDICATIONS						
	No Warnings	"Patient Sensitivity"	No Prophylaxis	Do Blood Studies	Blood Dyscrasias	No Trivial Infections[c]	"Chloramphenicol-indicated"	Prophylaxis[b]	Dysentery	Venereal Disease	Whooping Cough	Pneumonias	Typhoid Fever, Rocky Mt. Spotted Fever, H. Influenzae Meningitis[a]
UNITED STATES													
Chloromycetin – Parke-Davis (U.S.)			✓	✓	✓	✓							✓
UNITED KINGDOM													
Chloromycetin – Parke-Davis (U.S.)			✓	✓	✓	✓							✓
Kemicetine – Carlo Erba (Italy)			✓	✓	✓	✓							✓
AFRICA													
Adelcomycin – Adelco (Greece)			✓	✓	✓	✓							✓
Chloramex – Dumex (Denmark)			✓	✓	✓	✓							✓
Chlorocide – Medimpex (Hungary)			✓	✓	✓	✓							✓
Chloromycetin – Parke-Davis (U.S.)			✓	✓	✓	✓							✓
Chloromyk – Chropi (Greece)			✓	✓	✓	✓							✓
Comycetin – Cophar (Switzerland)			✓	✓	✓	✓							✓
Detreomycine – Polfa (Poland)			✓	✓	✓	✓							✓
Kemicetine – Carlo Erba (Italy)			✓	✓	✓	✓							✓
Niamycetine – R & N Pharmaceuticals (Greece)			✓	✓	✓	✓							✓

TABLE 2 continued

	INDICATIONS							WARNINGS					
	Typhoid Fever, Rocky Mt. Spotted Fever, H. Influenzae Meningitis[a]	Pneumonias	Whooping Cough	Venereal Disease	Dysentery	Prophylaxis[b]	"Chloramphenicol-indicated"	No Trivial Infections[c]	Blood Dyscrasias	Do Blood Studies	No Prophylaxis	"Patient Sensitivity"	No Warnings
Rivomycin – Rivopharm (Switzerland)	✓							✓	✓		✓		
Suismycetin – Lagap (Switzerland)	✓							✓	✓	✓	✓		
Synthomycetine – Lepetit/Dow Chemical (Italy/U.S.)	✓							✓	✓	✓	✓		
Tifomycine – Roussel (France)	✓							✓	✓	✓	✓		
INDONESIA													
Alchlor – Apex (Indonesia)	✓						✓ᵈ						✓
Aromycetin – Aroindo (Indonesia)	✓	✓	✓		✓		✓ᵈ						✓
Avicol – Konimex (Indonesia)							✓						✓
Chloramex – Dumex (Denmark)							✓						✓
Chloromycetin – Parke-Davis (U.S.)	✓						✓ᵈ						✓
Cloramidine – Arco (Indonesia)							✓ᵈ						✓
Colain – Kenrose (Indonesia)							✓ᵈ						✓
Colsancetine – Sanbe (Indonesia)	✓	✓	✓		✓		✓ᵈ		✓				✓
Combicetin – Combiphar (Indonesia)	✓						✓ᵈ						
Coromycetin – Coronet (Indonesia)							✓ᵈ						✓
Dellamycetin – Dupa (Indonesia)							✓						✓

TABLE 2 continued

	Typhoid Fever, Rocky Mt. Spotted Fever, H. Influenzae Meningitis[a]	Pneumonias	Whooping Cough	Venereal Disease	Dysentery	Prophylaxis[b]	"Chloramphenicol-indicated"	No Trivial Infections[c]	Blood Dyscrasias	Do Blood Studies	No Prophylaxis	"Patient Sensitivity"	No Warnings
	INDICATIONS							**WARNINGS**					
Denicol – D.E.F. Lab. (Indonesia)							✓		✓				✓
Ethimycetin – Ethica (Indonesia)							✓						✓
Fenicol – Conmed (Indonesia)							✓						✓
Kalmicetin – Kalbe Farma (Indonesia)							✓		✓				✓
Kemicetine – Carlo Erba (Italy)	✓	✓	✓		✓		✓[d]		✓				✓
Kunacol – Konimex (Indonesia)							✓		✓				✓
Librocetine – Bintang Toedjoe (Indonesia)							✓		✓				
Neophenicol – Westmont (Philippines)	✓		✓				✓[d]		✓				✓
Ottophenicol – Otto (Indonesia)							✓						✓
Paraphenicol – Prafa (Indonesia)							✓						✓
Paraxin – Boehringer Mannheim (W. Germany)			✓				✓[d]					✓	✓
Promycetin – I.P.I. (Indonesia)	✓						✓[d]						✓
Ribocine – Dexa (Indonesia)	✓						✓[d]						✓
Sammycin – Samco Farma (Indonesia)	✓		✓				✓[d]						✓
Scancetin – Scanchemie (Netherlands)	✓				✓		✓[d]						✓
Suprachlor – Meprofarm (Indonesia)	✓						✓[d]					✓	✓
Synthomycetine – Lepetit/Dow Chemical (Italy/U.S.)	✓						✓[d]						✓

TABLE 2 continued

	INDICATIONS							WARNINGS					
	Typhoid Fever, Rocky Mt. Spotted Fever, H. Influenzae Meningitis[a]	Pneumonias	Whooping Cough	Venereal Disease	Dysentery	Prophylaxis[b]	"Chloramphenicol-indicated"	No Trivial Infections[c]	Blood Dyscrasias	Do Blood Studies	No Prophylaxis	"Patient Sensitivity"	No Warnings
MALAYSIA/SINGAPORE													
Beaphenicol – Beacons (Singapore)	✓						✓[p]						✓
Enteromycetin – Zambon (Italy)	✓						✓[p]		✓				
Eucomycin – M.P.F. (Malaysia)	✓						✓[p]		✓				
Kemicetine – Carlo Erba (Italy)	✓						✓[p]		✓				
Synthomycetine – Lepetit/Dow Chemical (Italy/U.S.)			✓		✓		✓[p]		✓				
Ubicol – Little (Singapore), Antah Jardine Sandilands (Malaysia)	✓										✓		✓
Xepanicol – Xepa/Soul Pattinson (Malaysia/Singapore)	✓												✓
PHILIPPINES													
Biomycetin – Hizon (Philippines)	✓		✓	✓			✓[p]				✓	✓	✓
Carlophen – Interchem Labs (Philippines)				✓		✓	✓[p]			✓			
Catilan – Hoechst (W. Germany)						✓	✓[p]						
Chlorabicine – Abic/Inphilco (Israel/Philippines)	✓						✓[p]	✓					
Chloracol – Codisan A/S (Philippines)	✓						✓[p]	✓				✓	
Chloramed – Medicalex (Thailand)	✓						✓[p]	✓		✓		✓	

TABLE 2 continued

Product	WARNINGS						INDICATIONS						
	No Warnings	"Patient Sensitivity"	No Prophylaxis	Do Blood Studies	Blood Dyscrasias	No Trivial Infections[c]	"Chloramphenicol-indicated"[d]	Prophylaxis[b]	Dysentery	Venereal Disease	Whooping Cough	Pneumonias	Typhoid Fever, Rocky Mt. Spotted Fever, H. Influenzae Meningitis[a]
Chloramin – Uni-Med (Philippines)		✓		✓		✓	✓[d]						✓
Chloramphen – Oceanic (Philippines)		✓		✓		✓	✓[d]						✓
Chloromycetin – Parke-Davis (U.S.)				✓			✓[d]						✓
Cimycetin – Celchem (Hong Kong)		✓		✓			✓[d]						✓
Cloramidina – ICN/Arco (U.S.)		✓					✓[d]						✓
Dexophenicol – Medarex (Philippines)		✓		✓			✓[d]	✓	✓	✓		✓	✓
Enteromycetin – Zambon (Italy)	✓						✓[d]	✓				✓	✓
Germycetin – Rafgers (Philippines)		✓		✓			✓[d]		✓	✓			
Intermycetin – VCP Intermed (Philippines)	✓						✓[d]	✓	✓				✓
Kemicetine – Farmitalia Carlo Erba (Italy)		✓		✓			✓[d]	✓	✓				✓
Mycetin – Pharmazeutische Fabrik/Vonn Wälch (W. Germany)				✓			✓[d]			✓		✓	✓
Neophenicol – Westmont (Philippines)	✓						✓[d]		✓				
Pacimycetin – Pacific Pharm (Philippines)				✓			✓[d]						
Palmycetin – Systemics (Philippines)	✓						✓[d]						✓
Pediachlor – Pediatrica (Philippines)	✓						✓[d]						
Sanicol – Walter Ritter (W. Germany)		✓	✓	✓		✓	✓[d]				✓	✓	
Scanicol – Scandrug (Denmark)	✓						✓[d]		✓	✓			✓
Venimicetin – Doctors Pharm (Philippines)	✓						✓[d]		✓	✓			✓

TABLE 2 continued

	INDICATIONS							WARNINGS					
	Typhoid Fever, Rocky Mt. Spotted Fever, H. Influenzae Meningitis[a]	Pneumonias	Whooping Cough	Venereal Disease	Dysentery	Prophylaxis[b]	"Chloramphenicol-indicated"	No Trivial Infections[c]	Blood Dyscrasias	Do Blood Studies	No Prophylaxis	"Patient Sensitivity"	No Warnings
CENTRAL AMERICA													
Cloranfenicol-McKesson – McKesson (U.S.)	✓						✓	✓	✓	✓	✓	✓	
Cloranfenil – Collado (Dominican Republic)	✓						✓	✓	✓		✓	✓	
Chloromycetin – Parke-Davis (U.S.)	✓									✓			
Quemicetina – Montedison (Italy)	✓						✓[d]			✓			
Sintomicetina – Lepetit/Dow Chemical (Italy/U.S.)	✓						✓[d]		✓	✓			
Sopamycetin – Sopar (Belgium)							✓		✓	✓	✓		✓

Sources: The sources for the data presented in tables 2–8 are those described early in this chapter in the section headed Sources of Data.

[a] Also other severe infections when no other antibiotic is available.

[b] Usually prevention of surgical infections.

[c] Such as common cold, influenza, throat infections.

[d] Also such conditions as "genito-urinary tract infections," "gastrointestinal tract infections," "biliary infections," "respiratory tract infections," "ear, nose, and throat infections," "central nervous system infections," "surgical infections," "bacterial skin infections," "rickettsial diseases," "viral diseases," bronchitis, brucellosis, endocarditis, enterocolitis, gastroenteritis, laryngitis, laryngotracheitis, meningitis, peritonitis, plague, prostatitis, psittacosis, puerperal sepsis, septicemia, tonsillitis, trachoma, typhus, vaginitis, virus hepatitis.

Essentially the same recommendations and warnings are presented for Chloromycetin in *MIMS UK* and for three other chloramphenicol products marketed in Great Britain.

Similar restraint is apparent in the labeling of chloramphenicol products listed in *MIMS Africa*. In the Central African countries, it has been suggested, this uniformity in restraint—not apparent until recent years—has resulted not so much from a change in the promotional policies of the companies as from a new editorial policy established by *MIMS Africa*.

In Indonesia, Malaysia/Singapore, the Philippines, and Central America, physicians are given strikingly different information. Of the twenty-eight products listed here for Indonesia, all are accompanied by recommendations for use substantially broader than those shown in the United States, Great Britain, and Africa. Many of these indications concern conditions that could scarcely be viewed as life-threatening: diseases such as bronchitis, prostate infections, vaginal infections, and throat infections. In many instances, physicians are told essentially that the drug is indicated in conditions for which the drug is indicated—an imprecise guide offering little practical help to prescribers. With only six of these products is aplastic anemia or other devastating blood dyscrasia even mentioned in the listings, and none calls for blood studies. In the labeling of three-fourths of the products, *no* warnings whatsoever are given.

Approximately the same situation holds for Malaysia/Singapore. All but two of the seven products (the exceptions are Little/Antah Jardine Sandilands's Ubicol and Xepa/Soul Pattinson's Xepanicol) call for use in infections which are rarely if ever a threat to life. Three of the products, including Xepanicol, offer no warnings.

In the Philippines, none of the twenty-four products listed here carry recommendations for use only in life-threatening infections. Only five urge that the drug should not be administered for trivial infections. One-third of the products carry no warnings.

While Parke-Davis's Chloromycetin carries limited indications and precise warnings in the United States, Great Britain, and Africa, the same product is promoted with more indications and fewer warnings in the Philippines, and with more indications and no warnings in Indonesia. The promotion of the Parke-Davis product in Central America is essentially the same as it is in the United States or Great Britain. Similarly, Carlo Erba's Kemicetine carries limited indications and precise warnings in the United States, Great Britain, and Africa, but broader indications and limited warnings or none at all in Malaysia/Singapore and the Philippines.

It is frequently asserted by drug company officials that there is no real need to warn physicians of the dangers inherent in chloramphenicol. All health professionals are already aware of the problem, they insist, or easily get this information from the manufacturer. "Of course," a Sri Lanka physician says, "the company representative or detail man will tell you about the dangers—if you ask him. At least, I think he will."

A distinguished clinical pharmacologist told us of a pharmacist dying from chloramphenicol-induced aplastic anemia who asked, "Why didn't somebody tell me that this could happen?" And the physician who prescribed the drug for the pharmacist said, "But nobody warned me!"

Russel Chen, director of pharmacy at the National Taiwan University Hospital, says, "There is nothing in Taiwan law which requires a manufacturer to disclose these dangers to physicians and pharmacists. But if a poultry raiser buys chloramphenicol to use on his chickens, *he* gets the warnings. Is this reasonable? Is it even sane?"[27]

Tetracycline

Making their appearance at first in the late 1940s and early 1950s, members of the tetracycline family—chlortetracycline, oxytetracycline, later tetracycline itself, and their numerous derivatives—have won wide recognition as highly valuable drugs for the treatment of a great variety of infectious diseases. Thousands of derivatives have been examined, and many of these have been accepted for clinical use. At usual dosage levels, their toxicity is relatively low.

With only minor differences, the advantages and disadvantages of tetracycline itself are typical of those of its many relatives.

Clinical Background. Vast experience with tetracycline has demonstrated that it is effective in the treatment of dozens of different infective organisms. It may be used with remarkable safety in most adult men and in nonpregnant women. It may produce unpleasant but rarely serious gastrointestinal effects, including nausea, vomiting, and diarrhea. Infrequently, it may cause adverse effects on the blood and the skin. In some instances, its use has led to the rise and overgrowth of resistant strains of microorganisms, which usually can be controlled by another antibiotic.

Perhaps the most serious problem with tetracycline is linked to the development of kidney or liver disease, or its use in patients with impaired kidney or liver function. Such a use may result in death, and accordingly, physicians are urged to take appropriate precautions.

It has long been known that this antibiotic may permanently discolor teeth and interfere with bone growth in infants and children. For this reason, drug experts recommend that tetracycline should not be administered to women during the last half of pregnancy or to children under the ages eight to twelve unless there are "compelling reasons to do so."[28]

Promotion.   In this section, and in Table 3, attention is focused on four important warnings or contraindications which may—or may not—be provided to physicians. These include the use of tetracycline in the presence of kidney disease, in liver disease, during pregnancy, and in children.

In the United States, physicians are given this unambiguous warning in large type:

> THE USE OF DRUGS OF THE TETRACYCLINE CLASS DURING TOOTH DEVELOPMENT (LAST HALF OF PREGNANCY, INFANCY, AND CHILDHOOD TO THE AGE OF 8 YEARS) MAY CAUSE PERMANENT DISCOLORATION OF THE TEETH (YELLOW-GRAY-BROWN) . . . TETRACYCLINES SHOULD THEREFORE NOT BE USED IN THIS AGE GROUP UNLESS OTHER DRUGS ARE NOT LIKELY TO BE EFFECTIVE OR ARE CONTRAINDICATED.

Caution is likewise urged in the presence of kidney or liver impairment.

In *PDR*, such advice is prominently displayed in the labeling for Lederle's Achromycin, Robins's Robitet, Squibb's Sumycin, and Pfizer's Tetracyn. The drug, it is stated, should generally not be used in children up to the age of eight.

Roughly the same precautions are given to British physicians through *MIMS UK* for Lederle's Achromycin, M.C.P.'s Sustamycin, Organon's

	WARNINGS					
TABLE 3 **TETRACYCLINE** Products: Warnings	"Hypersensitivity" and Other	Caution in Kidney Disease	Caution in Liver Disease	Caution in Pregnancy	Minimum Age of Patient	No Specific Warnings
UNITED STATES						
Achromycin – Lederle (U.S.)	✔	✔	✔	✔	8 yrs.	
Robitet – Robins (U.S.)	✔	✔	✔	✔	8 yrs.	
Sumycin – Squibb (U.S.)	✔	✔	✔	✔	8 yrs.	
Tetracyn – Pfizer (U.S.)	✔	✔	✔	✔	8 yrs.	
UNITED KINGDOM						
Achromycin – Lederle (U.S.)	✔	✔	✔	✔	12 yrs.	
Sustamycin – M.C.P. (W. Germany)	✔	✔	✔	✔	12 yrs.	
Tetrabid – Organon (Netherlands)	✔	✔	✔	✔	12 yrs.	
Tetrachel – Berk/Revlon (U.K./U.S.)	✔	✔	✔	✔	12 yrs.	
Tetracyn – Pfizer (U.S.)	✔	✔	✔	✔	12 yrs.	
Totomycin – Boots (U.K.)	✔	✔	✔	✔	12 yrs.	
AFRICA						
Dumocycline – Dumex (Denmark)	✔	✔	✔	✔	12 yrs.	
Flavacyn – Boots (U.K.)	✔	✔	✔	✔	12 yrs.	
Hostacycline – Hoechst (W. Germany)	✔	✔	✔	✔	12 yrs.	
Nyacycline – R & N Pharmaceuticals (Greece)	✔	✔	✔	✔	12 yrs.	
Polfamycine – Polfa (Poland)	✔	✔	✔	✔	12 yrs.	
Retrivo – Rivopharm (Switzerland)	✔	✔	✔	✔	12 yrs.	
Robitet – Robins (U.S.)	✔	✔	✔	✔	12 yrs.	
Steclin – Squibb (U.S.)	✔	✔	✔	✔	12 yrs.	
Tetrafect – Berk/Revlon (U.K./U.S.)	✔	✔	✔	✔	12 yrs.	
Upcyclin – Cophar (Switzerland)	✔	✔	✔	✔	12 yrs.	
INDONESIA						
Achromycin – Lederle (U.S.)	✔					
Altetra – Apex (Indonesia)	✔					
Ambramycin – Lepetit/Dow Chemical (Italy/U.S.)						✔
Arocycline – Aroindo (Indonesia)						✔

TABLE 3 continued

	WARNINGS					
	"Hypersensitivity" and Other	Caution in Kidney Disease	Caution in Liver Disease	Caution in Pregnancy	Minimum Age of Patient	No Specific Warnings
Bekatetracyn – Kimla Farma (Indonesia)						✔
Centraclin – Centrafarm (Netherlands)						✔
Combicyclin – Combiphar (Indonesia)						✔
Conmycin – Conmed (Indonesia)						✔
Decyclin – D.E.F. Lab. (Indonesia)	✔					
Dellacyclin – Dupa (Indonesia)						✔
Dumocycline – Dumex (Denmark)					2 yrs.	
Enpicycline – Nicholas (Australia)	✔					
Ercyclin – Kimla Farma (Indonesia)						✔
Ethicacyn – Ethica (Indonesia)	✔					
Hi-Tetra – Mecosin (Indonesia)	✔	✔	✔			
Hostacycline – Hoechst (W. Germany)	✔	✔	✔	✔		
Intercyclin – Interbat (Indonesia)						✔
Kalcyclin – Kalbe Farma (Indonesia)						✔
Librocyn – Bintang Toedjoe (Indonesia)						✔
Meprotetra – Meprofarm (Indonesia)	✔					
Nelmicyn – Nellco (Indonesia)					1 yr.	
Ottocyclin – Otto (Indonesia)		✔	✔			
Panacyclin – I.P.I. (Indonesia)						✔
Samcycline – Samco Farma (Indonesia)						✔
Scantetra – Scanchemie (Netherlands)						✔
Spectrocycline – Westmont (Philippines)					2 yrs.	
Steclin – Squibb (U.S.)						✔
Sustamycin – Arco (Indonesia)	✔					
Tetracycline – Pharos (Indonesia)	✔					
Tetracyn – Pfizer (U.S.)	✔					
Tetradex – Dexa (Indonesia)						✔
Tetra Erba – Carlo Erba (Italy)						✔
Tetra "K" – Kenrose (Indonesia)						✔
Tetrarco – Arco (Indonesia)	✔					
Tetrasanbe – Sanbe (Indonesia)						✔
MALAYSIA/SINGAPORE						
Achromycin – Lederle (U.S.)	✔					

TABLE 3 continued

	WARNINGS					
	"Hypersensitivity" and Other	Caution in Kidney Disease	Caution in Liver Disease	Caution in Pregnancy	Minimum Age of Patient	No Specific Warnings
Ambramycin – Lepetit/Dow Chemical (Italy/U.S.)						✓
Beatacycline – Beacons (Singapore)						✓
Dumocycline – Dumex (Denmark)						✓
Hostacycline – Hoechst (W. Germany)		✓	✓	✓		
Panmycin – Upjohn (U.S.)	✓					
Pfizercycline (Tetracyn) – Pfizer (U.S.)	✓					
Pharmycin – MPF (Malaysia)						✓
Polfamycine – Ciech Polfa (Poland)						✓
Retifon – Roche (Switzerland)	✓					
Servitet – Servipharm/Ciba-Geigy (Switzerland)						✓
Systemacin – Pure/Summit (U.S.)						✓
Tetra – Asia Pharm (Philippines)		✓	✓			
Tetrerba – Carlo Erba (Italy)						✓
Vemyclin – Pharmmalaysia (Malaysia)						✓
Xepacycline – Xepa-Soul Pattinson (Singapore)						✓
PHILIPPINES						
Achromycin – Lederle (U.S.)	✓					
Alphacycline – Crovis Philcom (Italy)	✓					
Ambracyn – Biomedia (Italy)		✓			9 yrs.	
Cyclabid – Elan (Philippines)	✓					
Excelmycin – Excel (Philippines)		✓				
Filimycin – Filifarma (Philippines)	✓					
Fivecycline – Five-Med Labs (Philippines)				✓		
Geroxyl – Rafgers (Philippines)						✓
Hostacycline – Hoechst (W. Germany)	✓				9 yrs.	
Medicycline – Marcopharma (Thailand)	✓					
Mycristin – Purepac (U.S.)						✓
Otracyn – Mylan/Inphilco (U.S./Philippines)		✓	✓			
Pencycline – Codisan A/S (Philippines)					9 yrs.	

TABLE 3 continued	WARNINGS					
	"Hypersensitivity" and Other	Caution in Kidney Disease	Caution in Liver Disease	Caution in Pregnancy	Minimum Age of Patient	No Specific Warnings
Roracyn – Rorer (U.S.)						✔
Sautrex – Roche (Switzerland)[a]	✔					
Sumycin – Squibb (U.S.)		✔	✔			
Tetrabid – Organon (Netherlands)	✔	✔	✔		12 yrs.	
Tetrachlor – Otalco (Philippines)	✔					
Tetraclin – Oceanic (Philippines)	✔					
Tetracycline – UL Generics (Philippines)	✔					
Tetracycline – Upjohn (U.S.)	✔					
Tetracyn – Pfizer (U.S.)	✔					
Tetrad – Pharmagel (Philippines)				✔		
Tetrapoten – Scherer/Galenico (U.S./Philippines)						✔
Tetrarco – ICN/Arco (U.S.)	✔				12 yrs.	
Tetra-S – Scherer (U.S.)	✔					
Tetrerba – Carlo Erba (Italy)	✔					
Theracine – Rundell (Philippines)						✔
Tropicycline – Celchem (Hong Kong)				✔		
Wintrex – Winthrop-Stearns (U.S.)	✔					
CENTRAL AMERICA						
Acromicina – Lederle (U.S.)	✔	✔		✔		
Ambramicina – Lepetit/Dow Chemical (Italy/U.S.)	✔	✔	✔			
Dumocycline – Dumex (Denmark)					6 yrs.	
Steclin – Squibb (U.S.)	✔	✔		✔		
Tetraciclina-McKesson – McKesson (U.S.)	✔			✔		
Tetramin – Collado (Dominican Republic)				✔	8 yrs.	
Tetrex – Bristol (U.S.)						✔

[a] Not produced since 1979.

Tetrabid, Berk's Tetrachel, Pfizer's Tetracyn, and Boots's Totomycin. In Great Britain, however, physicians are warned against the administration of any tetracycline product in children up to the age of twelve.

Warnings identical to those presented in *MIMS UK* are given in *MIMS Africa* for Dumex's Dumocycline, Boots's Flavacyn, Hoechst's Hostacycline, R & N Pharmaceutical's Nyacycline, Polfa's Polfamycine, Robins's Robitet, Squibb's Steclin, Berk's Tetrafect, Rivopharm's Retrivo, and Cophar's Upcyclin.

In marked contrast, few specific warnings are given for the approximately 90 products described here for other developing countries. Thus warnings about use in kidney disease are given for only 13 of the products, about use in liver disease for only 9, and about use in pregnancy for only 9. No specific hazards of any kind are disclosed for 19 of the 35 products listed for Indonesia, 10 of the 16 for Malaysia/Singapore, 5 of the 30 for the Philippines, and 1 of the 7 for Central America. Where warnings are presented, most are vague, calling for "lower dosages" in children, noting that prolonged use may cause tooth discoloration and that there may be overgrowth of nonsusceptible organisms, or advising "see literature." Only infrequently, however, do physicians in developing countries ask to "see literature." Specific age limitations for treatment are suggested for only 10 of the 80-odd products, and these vary from twelve years to as low as one year or less. The fact that some of these clinically unjustifiable applications may be fatal is not mentioned.

For products marketed in two or more Third World areas, the warnings are often inconsistent. For example, reasonably full precautions are presented for Hoechst's Hostacycline in Africa, Indonesia, and Malaysia/Singapore, but not in the Philippines. The labeling for Polfa's Polfamycine contains full warnings in Africa, but none in Malaysia/Singapore. The approaches used for Lepetit's Ambramycin in Indonesia and Malaysia/Singapore are at least consistent: no hazards are disclosed in either area.

Lincomycin

Isolated from a mould found in soil collected near Lincoln, Nebraska, lincomycin has been applied—sometimes with remarkable results—in the control of serious infections caused by organisms resistant to penicillin, erythromycin, and other and safer antibiotics.

*Clinical Background.** American and British drug experts are in general agreement that lincomycin should be reserved for use in a few serious infections which cannot be effectively treated with safer drugs.[29]

The hazards involved in lincomycin therapy include severe and persistent diarrhea and the development of a severe and occasionally fatal form of colitis. The diarrhea may strike as many as 20 percent of treated patients. There may be nausea, abdominal cramps, and various hypersensitivity reactions. Physicians have been cautioned not to use the drug in patients with impaired liver or kidney function.

The risk of serious and potentially life-threatening adverse reactions, some authorities contend, is so great that lincomycin should be administered only to hospitalized patients.[30]

Promotion. The *PDR* description of lincomycin, marketed by Upjohn under the name of Lincocin, begins with this precaution:

> WARNING—Lincomycin can cause severe colitis which may end fatally. Therefore, it should be reserved for serious infections where less toxic antimicrobial agents are inappropriate. . . . It should not be used in patients with nonbacterial infections, such as most respiratory tract infections.

American physicians are urged to be cautious in using the drug in older patients and in patients with a history of gastrointestinal disease, asthma, or other significant allergies. In patients undergoing prolonged therapy, periodic liver-function tests and blood counts should be performed.

In Great Britain, prescribers are told that Lincocin is indicated for serious lincomycin-sensitive infections. Use should be discontinued if persistent diarrhea or colitis appears. In newborn infants, liver function and blood counts should be checked regularly during prolonged treatments. There is no mention that the colitis may end in death.

In *MIMS Africa,* the risk of colitis—whether mild or potentially fatal—is not disclosed.

In the descriptions for Indonesia, Malaysia/Singapore, and Central America, physicians are cautioned against administration of lincomycin

*The clinical background and the promotional approaches described here apply in general also to clindamycin, a related antibiotic marketed by Upjohn under such names as Cleocin and Dalacin C.

to newborn infants, or to patients with kidney, liver, endocrine, or metabolic disease. It is not recommended for the prevention of recurrent
rheumatic fever. It should be used cautiously in pregnant women. But
the possible occurrence of severe and potentially fatal colitis is not disclosed. In the Philippines, the labeling includes the statement that Lincocin "may cause G.I. disorder." Neither the kind of gastrointestinal
disorder nor the possibility of a fatal outcome is mentioned.

Combination Antibiotics

Almost since the start of the antibiotic era, pharmaceutical companies
have offered physicians a wide array of two or more of these drugs in
fixed combination. The logic behind the use of these products is not
always clear. They often offered convenience. In some cases, they were
proposed for use when the disease apparently was caused by what are
known as "mixed infections." In others, the combinations seemed war-
ranted in severe infections when no precise diagnosis could be made,
when the nature of the causative organism was unknown, or to delay
the appearance of resistant strains. Or, in some instances, use of the
combination was supported by the notion that if one antibiotic was
good, two or more in combination must be better. There was sometimes
the dangerous notion that even if the second component wouldn't help,
it couldn't hurt.

Regardless of the underlying reasons, the commercial success of combination antibiotics was obvious. At one time or another, they represented roughly one-half of all antibiotic prescriptions—and, in some developing countries, they still do.[31] It seems difficult to determine
whether the popularity of combination antibiotics was the result of their
supposed clinical advantages or of the massive promotional campaigns
mounted by the drug companies.

Although the actual values of the combinations had been questioned
increasingly for more than a decade, the subject came under full-scale
analysis beginning in the late 1960s and early 1970s. Acting under a
new policy laid down by the U.S. Congress, the Food and Drug Administration undertook a large program to reevaluate virtually all new
drugs introduced between 1938 and 1962.[32] (Presumably, all drugs put
on the U.S. market after 1962 had been studied for both safety and
efficacy, as was required by the Kefauver-Harris Amendments of 1962.)

In the Drug Efficacy Study set up by FDA, expert panels of the prestigious National Academy of Sciences/National Research Council attempted to classify all prescription drugs into a number of different categories: "effective," "probably effective," "possibly effective," "ineffective," and "effective but. . . ." This last group was used to include those products which were found effective for some of the applications claimed by the manufacturer, but not for all of them, and which therefore required a change in labeling and promotion.

In addition, one other category was found necessary: "ineffective as a fixed combination." It was probably not a happy choice of words, but the panel members knew what the term was supposed to mean. It covered fixed-combination products—including not only antibiotics but also other drugs—whose individual components were unquestionably effective and relatively safe when used individually, but whose use in combination form represented less efficacy or less safety or both.

In the panel hearings, expert witnesses testified that fixed-ratio combinations were formulated arbitrarily by the manufacturer and not to meet the needs of an individual patient. In some cases, it was charged, the presence of the second ingredient could interfere with the absorption or the actions of the first. Administering the two drugs in combination often made it impossible to set up an appropriate dosage schedule for each component. If the patient developed an adverse reaction, it would be difficult if not impossible to determine quickly which ingredient was responsible.

For these and other reasons, FDA was urged to remove every combination antibiotic product from the market as "ineffective as a fixed combination." In drug industry circles, where combination antibiotics were considered to be particularly lucrative, the proposed move was bitterly opposed. FDA officials were denounced for interfering in the practice of medicine, for limiting the right of physicians to prescribe as they saw fit, for threatening the sacrosanct "doctor-patient relationship," and—presumably as a consequence—sentencing American patients to receive only second-class medical care.

In the years of furious debate, much of the anti-FDA attack was spearheaded by two powerful firms, Upjohn and Squibb. Upjohn was the producer of Albamycin T, a combination of tetracycline and novobiocin, while Squibb was marketing Mysteclin F, composed of tetracycline and amphotericin. Both were highly successful commercially. Both were warmly supported by some individual physicians, many of whom testified to the effect that "I can't practice medicine without it."

It appeared later that many of these endorsements were written by a friendly detail man who would borrow the necessary office stationery from a physician, type a standard letter—often with the identical spelling, punctuation, and spacing—and then ask the physician merely to sign the document. It also appeared that the combination was often more toxic than either ingredient used alone. The combinations, most drug experts concluded, possessed few if any significant clinical advantages.

After prolonged disputes and litigation, the courts finally ruled in favor of FDA, and combination antibiotics were removed from the U.S. market. So far as experts on infectious disease can determine, the health of Americans has not visibly suffered. In the United Kingdom, some combinations—notably Albamycin T and Mysteclin F—have continued in use, but most have disappeared. British drug authorities have evidently agreed with their American colleagues, but only up to a point. In most developing countries, the promotion and the popularity of these products continue unabated, even though many carry excessive prices.

Clinical Background. The ratios for fixed-ratio combination antibiotic products were originally established by the manufacturers on the basis of *in vitro* or test-tube measurements. These, it has been found, have correlated "very poorly" with clinical results in patients. Mixtures of these agents, most experts feel, have turned out to be superior to a single antibiotic in only a very few instances. Such agreement now casts an embarrassing light on the testimonials of physicians who once testified that they "couldn't practice medicine without it."

Louis Weinstein, of Tufts, Harvard, and Boston College, put the matter in these words:

> The readiness and enthusiasm with which the claims made for such mixtures have been accepted are remarkable because, with few exceptions, there is a striking lack of critically evaluated and carefully controlled data in support of their use in the treatment of disease.[33]

The convenience of these combination products, it has been noted, may be greatly outweighed by the dangers of inappropriate or excessive dosage, hypersensitivity to one ingredient of the combination, or administration of superfluous drugs. The risk to small or elderly patients, or those with impaired liver or kidney function, is particularly great. There is little justification for their use.[34]

Promotion. Except for several sulfa-drug-containing products and for products intended solely for external use, combination antibiotic products are no longer listed in the American *PDR,* and few remain in the British *MIMS.*

In developing countries, scores of these products are still promoted, prescribed, and used. Among them are such combinations as these:

— chloramphenicol with streptomycin or tetracycline

— tetracycline with amphotericin, novobiocin, nystatin, or oleandomycin

— penicillin with streptomycin

— ampicillin with cloxacillin

In this section, consideration is given only to the chloramphenicol-containing combinations listed for developing countries, and only to the hazards, contraindications, and warnings disclosed to physicians (see Table 4).

In the case of the three products listed for Africa, fair to reasonably complete warnings are presented for all. No warnings are given for any of the six combinations listed for Indonesia. Of the eight products listed for the Philippines, six give partial warnings. Incomplete warnings are provided for the two products listed in Central America.

Particularly where chloramphenicol is involved, inadequate warnings or no warnings at all may result needlessly in injury or death.

DRUGS AGAINST DIARRHEA

For countless centuries, people in most of the world—all of Africa except parts of South Africa, all of South and Central America and Mexico, essentially all of Asia, the southern portions of Europe, and even the glamorous islands of the tropics—have been plagued by the family of dysenteric diseases.

Most of these ailments are only briefly uncomfortable or incapacitat-

TABLE 4
Chloramphenicol-Containing
COMBINATION ANTIBIOTICS:
Warnings

	WARNINGS								
	As for Chloramphenicol	No Trivial Infections	Blood Dyscrasias	Do Blood Studies	No Prophylaxis	As for Streptomycin	As for Tetracycline	Caution During Pregnancy	No Warnings
AFRICA									
Ambrasynth – Lepetit/Dow Chemical (Italy/U.S.) (chloramphenicol + tetracycline)			✓				✓		
Chlorostrept – Parke-Davis (U.S.) (chloramphenicol + streptomycin)		✓	✓		✓	✓			
Kemi-Cycline – Carlo Erba (Italy) (chloramphenicol + tetracycline)		✓	✓	✓	✓		✓		
INDONESIA									
Bekachlorocyn – Kimia Farma (Indonesia) (chloramphenicol + tetracycline)									✓
Dexacyclin – Dexa (Indonesia) (chloramphenicol + tetracycline)									✓
Kemicycline – Carlo Erba (Italy) (chloramphenicol + tetracycline)									✓

TABLE 4 continued

	WARNINGS								
	No Warnings	Caution During Pregnancy	As for Tetracycline	As for Streptomycin	No Prophylaxis	Do Blood Studies	Blood Dyscrasias	No Trivial Infections	As for Chloramphenicol
Levocyclin – Combiphar (Indonesia) (chloramphenicol + tetracycline)	✓								
Scanstrepchlor – Scanchemie (Netherlands) (chloramphenicol + dihydrostreptomycin)	✓								
Tetra Colme – Interbat (Indonesia) (chloramphenicol + tetracycline)	✓								
PHILIPPINES									
Chloramphenicol/Streptomycin – UL Generics (Philippines) (chloramphenicol + streptomycin)									✓
Chloram-Strep – Codisan A/S (Philippines) (chloramphenicol + streptomycin)									✓
Chlorostrep – Parke-Davis (U.S.) (chloramphenicol + streptomycin)						✓		✓	
Dostrol – United American (Philippines) (chloramphenicol + streptomycin)									✓

TABLE 4 continued

	As for Chloramphenicol	No Trivial Infections	Blood Dyscrasias	Do Blood Studies	No Prophylaxis	As for Streptomycin	As for Tetracycline	Caution During Pregnancy	No Warnings
Entrecin – Westmont (Philippines) (chloramphenicol + streptomycin)				✓					
Kemistrep – Farmitalia Carlo Erba (Italy) (chloramphenicol + streptomycin)				✓					
Marcomycin – Marcopharma (Denmark) (chloramphenicol + streptomycin)									✓
Venistrep – Doctors Pharm (Philippines) (chloramphenicol + streptomycin)									✓
CENTRAL AMERICA									
Ambrasinto – Lepetit/Dow Chemical (Italy/U.S.) (chloramphenicol + tetracycline)				✓					
Quemiciclina – Montedison (Italy) (chloramphenicol + tetracycline)			✓				✓		

ing. In uncommon but serious forms, such as amebic dysentery, they can be seriously disabling for weeks or months and sometimes fatal. They strike not only native populations but also unwary tourists or visiting businessmen, and sometimes invading armies.

The areas involved are the do-not-drink-the-water countries. Sanitation and sewage control are largely or entirely nonexistent, and most water supplies and uncooked foods are contaminated.

Accordingly, in these countries, drugs to treat diarrhea and dysentery have an importance that cannot be appreciated by those who spend their whole lives in developed parts of the world. For those who live in the Third World, such antidiarrheal agents are among the most widely used of all medicines. Unfortunately, the potential hazards of some of them have not been so widely appreciated—nor widely mentioned.

Clioquinol

In the early 1930s, a new drug now known as clioquinol was developed by a group of scientists headed by Hamilton Anderson and Norman David at the University of California in San Francisco. It was tested mainly for the treatment of amebic dysentery, a field in which the UC group had long been working. In 1934, it was introduced for marketing by the Swiss firm Ciba (now Ciba-Geigy) primarily for amebic dysentery. Nevertheless, within a few years, and without the knowledge and consent of the Californians, it was being promoted and used for the control of virtually all types of dysentery. It was known originally as Vioform or Entero-Vioform.

In those early years, the drug was generally assumed to be not merely remarkably effective but also remarkably safe. Since it was accepted that clioquinol was almost insoluble and not absorbed from the intestinal tract into the rest of the body, there seemed to be no way in which it might damage or even influence the rest of the body.

In the late 1950s, however, Japanese physicians began reporting the appearance of what appeared to be a brand-new condition now called SMON, for subacute-myelo-optico-neuropathy—a dreadful name but a far more dreadful disease. This was the beginning of what has become known in some circles as the Entero-Vioform horror.

Victims generally suffered first from tingling, next a loss of sensation, and then paralysis of both feet and legs. In many cases, there were violent gastrointestinal effects, often including diarrhea and severe abdominal pain. Many victims suffered from visual disturbances which sometimes led to total blindness. Some patients died. Many of the changes were incurable, irreversible, and permanent.

Eventually, in Japan alone, more than 10,000 documented cases were reported. Hospitals were jammed with victims of the epidemic, and new wards had to be built to accommodate them. It was apparently the worst drug disaster in history.

What was the cause of this catastrophic new plague? Blame was put on vitamin deficiencies, metabolic defects, agricultural insecticides, and contaminated water—all without supporting evidence. For a number of years, the sudden appearance of SMON led some scientists to suspect an infectious agent, most probably a virus, as the offending agent. The claim that a "SMON virus" had actually been isolated brought sensational newspaper headlines. The "SMON virus" concept did little to comfort the patients. Some of them, perhaps from the painful symptoms and some from fear that they might infect other family members, committed suicide.

Then, in 1970, there came strong evidence that SMON was caused by—or associated with—Entero-Vioform. Many Japanese, it seemed, had been accustomed to using this drug not only to treat diarrhea of every conceivable variety but also to prevent it. To the Japanese, with their traditional preoccupation with all digestive disorders, the drug was accepted as *seichozai*, a kind of "digestive stabilizer." It was swallowed daily by thousands of people for months or years.

Says one modern SMON expert, "People took it—and physicians prescribed it—as if it were some kind of benevolent vitamin for the intestinal tract."

In September of 1970, even though the chain of evidence was not yet complete, the Japanese government felt that the case was strong enough to justify a ban on all sales of Entero-Vioform and 185 similar products that had come on the market. The companies—Ciba-Geigy in particular—were not visibly pleased with this development. Company spokesmen insisted that the drug was unquestionably safe, that it had been used without any problems on millions of patients all over the world for more than thirty years. They emphasized that clioquinol could not conceivably cause bodily injury or death because it was essentially insoluble and therefore could not be absorbed into the body.

To many Japanese physicians, this whole disaster was unbelievable. At a 1979 conference, one leading doctor asked:

How could this have happened? If only we had known that the drug could have such terrible effects, we would never have prescribed it. Why didn't anybody tell us? Why weren't we warned?

But the physicians and pharmacists could have been warned. The warning signs had been present from the outset. In their first reports on clioquinol, later confirmed by others, the University of California scientists demonstrated that even though clioquinol and similar compounds were *relatively* insoluble, they were not *completely* insoluble. They could be absorbed into the body. They could produce liver damage. They could kill experimental animals. And how could these substances damage the liver without being absorbed?

In 1935, only a year after Entero-Vioform appeared on the market, P. Busse Grawitz and Enrique Barros announced from Argentina that they had tried the drug on patients and that each had observed a patient who developed strange signs of bilateral nerve damage.

In 1944, Norman David and his co-workers, who had moved from San Francisco to the University of Oregon, pointed to their findings on animals and warned that the use of drugs like clioquinol in the prevention of amebic dysentery "must be rigidly controlled and should not be carried out as extensively or as freely as is done in the prophylaxis of malaria with quinine."[35]

Even in the case of treatment rather than prevention, David wrote in the *Journal of the American Medical Association,* the therapy should be limited to a short period of ten to fourteen days.[36]

"Furthermore," Anderson told us recently, "we were talking only about amebic dysentery. Other types of dysentery or diarrhea usually terminate—with or without treatment—in about three or four days."[37]

Other investigators failed to find evidence that clioquinol was even useful against the common forms of dysentery or what is sometimes called "traveler's diarrhea" or "summer diarrhea." A study conducted on American students who had gone to Mexico showed that "traveler's diarrhea" afflicted only about 20 percent of those who had taken a different anti-infective substance, novobiocin, as a preventive, 34 percent of those who had taken a placebo or "dummy pills," and nearly 39 percent of those who took clioquinol.[38] Swedish scientists working with people who had gone on vacation to Mediterranean countries later reported similar results.

Further evidence came from a Swiss veterinarian, Paul Hangartner, who was called upon to treat pets that had been given clioquinol for diarrhea. These animals developed acute epileptic-like convulsions and some had died. Swedish investigators independently made the same observations.[39]

"Ciba failed to mention that it had made similar observations in animal experiments 23 years before, in 1939," declared Olle Hansson, a Swedish pediatrician at the University of Göteborg. These reports, he added, "did not provoke the drug companies to investigate whether this also happened in humans. They simply denied it."[40]

Ciba did, however, notify veterinarians that Entero-Vioform should no longer be used on animals.

Hansson and his co-worker, Lennart Berggren, an ophthalmologist at the University of Uppsala, proceeded to undertake their own study on a human subject. Working with a three-year-old boy who had been treated with clioquinol and whose vision had been seriously affected, they found that clioquinol could be detected in the child's urine.[41] "There was no way," they said afterwards, "that clioquinol could have appeared in the urine unless it first had been absorbed out of the intestinal tract and into the body."

In Japan, investigators had observed for many years that some SMON patients developed a peculiar green discoloration of the surface of the tongue. The same green pigment occasionally appeared in the feces and even in the urine. In June of 1970, Zenzo Tamura of the University of Tokyo identified the green pigment as a metallic conjugation product of Entero-Vioform.[42] Quickly, neurologist Tadao Tsubaki checked the records of SMON patients and found that, in most cases, the victims had taken Entero-Vioform or some other clioquinol product before their symptoms had appeared. (Ciba-Geigy officials said later that their scientists had failed to find any trace of Entero-Vioform in the urine, but confessed that the scientists had used the wrong method of analysis.)[43] Although the evidence was not complete, it was enough to convince the Japanese team that clioquinol was the cause of SMON.[44]

Meanwhile, the promotion of clioquinol products—not simply for the treatment of the serious amebic dysentery but for the prevention of the amebic form of the disease and both the prevention and the treatment of other kinds of dysentery—continued in most countries without substantial abatement.

In Japan, according to public health expert Toshio Higashida of Kansai Medical University, Japanese physicians continued to be told by company literature or company representatives:

— *It is a safe and effective drug.*

— *It has no side effects.*

— *It is hardly absorbed from the intestines.*

— *Any side effect is temporary, so the prescription need not be discontinued.*

— *It is even safe for children.*[45]

In Sweden, at least up to 1966, Ciba-Geigy told physicians that Entero-Vioform is "tolerated extremely well even with long-term use."[46]

In Great Britain, an enterprising Ciba official designed a "Family Pack" containing 100 tablets of Entero-Vioform, apparently designed for Britons about to go on vacation. The package leaflet contained this advice:

> For the prevention and treatment of holiday diarrhoeas. . . . For diarrhoea winter and summer. . . . The whole year round for treatment of diarrhoea caused by winter sickness, gastroenteritis, food poisoning and intestinal complaints.[47]

The drug, travelers were told, should be taken each day as a preventive measure, starting from "the day on which you leave home."

On the back of the leaflet were such helpful hints as how much to tip in various foreign countries and the continental equivalents of British sizes of shoes, socks, and other items of clothing. (Such a Family Pack was purchased at a pharmacy in London in January 1977.) These instructions did, however, contain this message: "Note: This formulation is not suitable for treatment of animals."

As early as 1960 in the United States, FDA experts were already expressing doubts about the safety and efficacy of Entero-Vioform in common diarrhea. They advised that the drug should no longer be sold over the counter but instead should be dispensed only on a physician's prescription for amebic dysentery. Regardless of Ciba's protestations,

FDA noted that chemical relatives of Entero-Vioform could be absorbed at least in small amounts from the intestinal tract and that Entero-Vioform might also be absorbed. In 1961, Ciba agreed to modify its labeling. In 1972, the drug was removed completely from the U.S. market, not by FDA order but because of what Ciba-Geigy spokesmen described cryptically as "economic reasons."

In the United Kingdom, at least in part because of editorial warnings expressed in leading medical journals, Entero-Vioform was banned as an over-the-counter remedy but allowed to remain on the market as a prescription drug. This encouraged some drug salesmen to assert that the medicine could not be particularly dangerous, since it still could be prescribed in England. What the salesmen had neglected to note is that, somehow or other, Entero-Vioform and similar products are *not* being prescribed (except for external use) for British patients, and these products are no longer promoted or listed in *MIMS UK*.

A few other countries, notably Sweden, the Netherlands, Australia, France, and India, have either banned clioquinol or rigidly controlled its use. In some countries, company officials have attempted to minimize dangers by recommending that the drug should be used for a limited period, generally 28 days (usually three 250-mg tablets or capsules per day). But a recent survey by the London *Sunday Times* found that the maximum period of therapy is shown by Ciba-Geigy as 21 days in Greece, 24 days in Indonesia, 28 days in Spain and Austria, and 56 days in Italy.[48]

In Japan, the government's ban on clioquinol products in 1970 was followed in 1971 by the first of a barrage of unprecedented damage suits. Through their attorneys, the patients or their parents, children, or other survivors called for compensation to reimburse them for medical and hospital care, and—in the case of those no longer able to work or care for themselves—for support. Among the defendants were not only Ciba-Geigy and such Japanese firms as Takeda and Tanabe but also the Japanese government. The plaintiffs told the Japanese government essentially this: *You were supposed to protect our health. You failed to do so. You should pay damages.*

The suits, which dragged on in the courts for many years, were bitterly contested by both the defendant industries and the government. Experts testified that Entero-Vioform and similar products had been used in Japan for nearly forty years without any signs of injury, and that therefore the drugs could not be regarded as unsafe. (This is the familiar "test of time" argument used repeatedly in the United States in attempts to block FDA's implementation of the 1962 Kefauver-Harris Amendments—an argument that was finally rejected by the United States Supreme Court.)

There were claims that SMON was "a Japanese disease, a Japanese problem," because practically no cases had occurred outside of Japan. The blame, it was argued, must therefore be placed not on the drug companies but on some unidentified genetic weakness or other flaw among the Japanese. But although Japan was hit with the bulk of the SMON cases, other countries did not completely escape the disaster; cases have now been reported from the United States (only a very few), Sweden, Norway, Denmark, the United Kingdom, the Netherlands, France, West Germany, Indonesia, Switzerland, Australia, India, and other nations.[49] So far as we can determine, no confirmed cases have been reported in Sri Lanka, Malaysia, Taiwan, Korea, Israel, or any African nation. The fact that no cases were reported from some countries, however, may mean that no cases occurred or that none were diagnosed.

During the trials in Japan, much was made of the possibility that SMON was actually caused by a virus or some other infectious agent, and that therefore no drug could be properly blamed. This infectious-cause concept was never particularly persuasive to most medical experts. In very few cases did the disease strike two or more individuals in the same family. In some curious instances, the disease seemed to follow a particular prescriber; for example, one physician avidly prescribed Entero-Vioform in one hospital, in which many of his patients became afflicted with SMON, but when he was transferred to another hospital, the SMON epidemic vanished from the first hospital and broke out in the second.[50] Perhaps what did most to demolish the infectious-cause notion was the finding that, at just about the same time that all clioquinol drugs were banned from Japan, the SMON epidemic in Japan virtually disappeared.

Many of the developments described above were laid out in great and sometimes shocking detail in 1979 before an international audience of drug experts at the Kyoto International Conference on Drug Induced Sufferings (KICADIS). It was the opening of what KICADIS leaders said was "a worldwide campaign to see that this kind of horror never happens again, anywhere in the world."

Although not all the litigation in the Japanese courts has been completed, the verdicts have been handed down in many cases. In June 1976, even before the decisions were rendered, the outcome might have been predicted; the companies—probably recognizing that they were facing defeat—asked the court to recommend a settlement. At the end, all of the defendants—including the government—were found guilty and told to pay.

In 1981, a team of attorneys summed up the situation in Japan:

> SMON litigation has continued for a full ten years since the first case was brought to court on May 28, 1971.... As of May 1, 1981, of the 6,048 patients who brought their cases to court, it has been determined that 5,039 of them are suffering from SMON, and 4,734 of them have obtained settlements resulting in the payment of a total of 109,346,000,000 yen in damages.... Ciba-Geigy had been aware that many harmful side-effects of the drug had been reported since as early as 1935.[51]

The amount was equivalent to approximately $490 million, almost certainly the largest such settlement ever awarded in any country. Roughly one-third was paid by the Japanese government, the remainder by Ciba-Geigy and two Japanese drug companies. Some 1,300 additional cases were still pending in Japan. The Japanese lawyers and their clients agreed that a substantial amount of the award would be allocated to a worldwide program of information and education to assure that this kind of drug disaster would never reoccur.

In Sweden, forty-three cases have been settled.[52] Suits in other countries are yet to come to trial. In addition, a suit was filed in London against Squibb by an American woman who claimed that her blindness and paralysis were caused by a related drug, Quixalin. No verdict was reached, since Squibb agreed during the hearing in 1981 to settle out of court.[53]

The litigation may have provided a legal end to part of the SMON problem but not to all of it. To scientists, there remain some questions that have not yet been answered:

— Why did SMON—or what was diagnosed as SMON—afflict some

Japanese patients who apparently never took any clioquinol? Was it that they did not take the drug, or their medical reports were incomplete, or the patients themselves did not know which drug they had been given, or did not remember?

— Why is there an apparently enormous disparity in the rates of SMON in various countries? Is there, in fact, a defect in the Japanese gene pool that carries a susceptibility to the disease?

— Why did no cases appear among the many hundreds of patients treated in California?

— Is clioquinol *the* cause of SMON or *a* cause?

It should be noted, however, that similar puzzles—many of them still unsolved—have occurred with other medical problems.

There is a footnote that deserves recording, one that indicates the manner in which some drug company representatives have reacted to all these developments. In the spring of 1980, with the courageous support of her editors, young Dorothy Kweyu of the Nairobi *Sunday Nation* in Kenya wrote an article noting that Entero-Vioform and other clioquinol products had been implicated as a cause of SMON and was available, sometimes without prescription, in Kenyan pharmacies. She was summoned to meet with three officials of Ciba-Geigy and one of the company's local publicity representatives. The meeting was tape-recorded.[54] The Ciba representatives quickly expressed to her their displeasure with her article and particularly with the fact that she had not submitted it to Ciba for review before it was printed.

The Ciba-Geigy policy was clearly enunciated: "In view of the very low number of neurological disturbances reported from outside Japan in association with clioquinol therapy, we remain of the opinion that another factor or factors must have played a role in the occurrence of the SMON in Japan between 1955 and 1970." Among such factors, they said, could be an infectious agent, a vitamin deficiency, mercury or other heavy-metal contaminants in drinking water, or agricultural or industrial pollutants.

"During the introduction stage," the Ciba-Geigy representatives said, "all possible clinical trials were conducted in animals, in human volunteers, and it was concluded by the medical department that it was safe for human consumption."

The reporter asked, "Am I wrong to suggest that at the time this case came up in the Japanese courts, Ciba-Geigy already had experiments, documents pertaining to the fact that the drug caused convulsions and even deaths in dogs?"

"Yes, this is very true," the company representative replied. "But what does this say? . . . A drug which is perfectly safe for human beings can be deadly to dogs and cats."

Kweyu continued, "Okay, Doctor, let's go on. Why did the Ciba-Geigy company decide or agree to pay compensation for the victims of clioquinol?"

"Let me ask you, do you interpret the fact that we paid compensation as an admission of guilt?"

"Exactly."

The Ciba-Geigy representative said, "The payment is an admission that some SMON patients had clioquinol side effects. . . . We do not admit that clioquinol causes SMON. . . . It is an admission that among the SMON patients there were cases with clioquinol side effects." Further, he told the reporter, "It would be possible to fight and fight and fight, and kind of prolong the whole court cases until the last SMON patient has finally died." But Ciba-Geigy would not do such a thing because "we have a moral and ethical responsibility."

Whether or not SMON should or should not be viewed as a side effect may be—and probably will be—argued interminably by company spokesmen. The important point, however, seems to be that Ciba-Geigy paid, not because it *felt* responsible, but because the courts *found* the company responsible.

The Ciba-Geigy representatives who, as late as 1980 or 1981, were still insisting on the innocence of the drug, have evidently decided to overlook Ciba's formal admission made in writing through the Japanese courts to the Japanese SMON victims:

> Since the beginning of this lawsuit, the plaintiffs and their representatives have told the court of many sufferings caused by the SMON disease. It has been repeatedly stressed that only a SMON patient can truly understand his fellow patients' sufferings. We believe that we must solemnly accept their grievances. We who manufactured and sold clioquinol drugs deeply sympathize with the plaintiffs and their families in their continuing unbelievable agony; there are no words to adequately express our sorrow. *In view of the fact that medical products manufactured and*

sold by us have been responsible for the occurrence of the tragedy in Japan, we extend our apologies, frankly and without reservation to the plaintiffs and their families.[55]

The apology was dated December 9, 1979. It will not alleviate any paralysis or blindness, but at least it is on the record.

Clinical Background. After more than ten years of controversy ranging from vehement to violent, and involving physicians, pharmacologists, virus experts, epidemiologists, industry spokesmen, government officials, attorneys, and the SMON victims themselves, there now appears to be reasonable agreement among British and American authorities. Clioquinol, they say, is indicated solely for use in the treatment of amebic dysentery or intestinal amebiasis, although some investigators have recently reported that the drug is appropriate in the treatment of bacillary dysentery.[56]

Although clioquinol is practically insoluble in water, absorption from the intestinal tract does occur. Administration should be limited to a period of ten days. With prolonged use of high dosages, and sometimes with even normal amounts, there may be nerve damage and optic atrophy.[57] "Large doses, even when taken for short periods, may cause SMON," it has been emphasized.[58]

The risk in no way justifies continued clioquinol use for any condition other than amebic dysentery. There is no evidence, they agree, that the drug is effective in the prevention of "traveler's diarrhea" or similar conditions. Its indiscriminate use must be criticized. The argument that clioquinol is safe and effective because "it has been used for many decades on millions of people" is dismissed as being without merit.

Promotion. From Table 5 it is apparent that the proposed indications for use noted in the previous section—only for treatment of amebic dysentery—have not been accepted in the Third World countries. In all the areas considered here, most manufacturers recommend use of their products in a wide and sometimes vague assortment of conditions.

There is a similar lack of consistency in the presentation of warnings. No warnings are given for 2 of the 8 products listed for Africa, 9 of the 13 for Indonesia, or any of the 6 products for Malaysia/Singapore or the 3 for the Philippines.

A limit on the duration of treatment is given for only the Ciba-Geigy

TABLE 5

CLIOQUINOL

Products: Indications and Warnings

	INDICATIONS						WARNINGS				
	Amebic Dysentery	Bacillary Dysentery	Diarrhea	"Traveler's Diarrhea," "Summer Diarrhea"	Enteritis & Enterocolitis	"Gastrointestinal Infections"	Maximum No. Days of Treatment	Sensitivity to Iodine, Hyperthyroidism	Caution in Kidney, Liver Disease	Optic, Other Nerve Damage	No Warnings
UNITED STATES None listed											
UNITED KINGDOM Some products for external use only											
AFRICA											
Ente-Rivo Simplex – Rivopharm (Switzerland)	✓	✓	✓		✓	✓					✓
Enteromycin – Medinova (Switzerland)	✓	✓	✓		✓	✓					✓
Enterosüiss – Lagap (Switzerland)			✓			✓					
Entero-Vioform – Ciba-Geigy (Switzerland)							28	✓	✓		
Entox – Wyeth (U.S.)					✓			✓	✓		
Mebinol – Carlo Erba (Italy)					✓			✓	✓		
Mexaform – Ciba-Geigy (Switzerland)					✓	✓	28	✓	✓		✓
Nimarol – Ciba-Geigy (Switzerland)					✓	✓	28	✓	✓		
INDONESIA											
Diarent – Kenrose (Indonesia)	✓	✓	✓		✓						✓

TABLE 5 continued

	WARNINGS					INDICATIONS					
	No Warnings	Optic, Other Nerve Damage	Caution in Kidney, Liver Disease	Sensitivity to Iodine, Hyperthyroidism	Maximum No. Days of Treatment	"Gastrointestinal Infections"	Enteritis & Enterocolitis	"Traveler's Diarrhea," "Summer Diarrhea"	Diarrhea	Bacillary Dysentery	Amebic Dysentery
Enterosept – Soho (Indonesia)	✓					✓			✓	✓	✓
Entero-Vioform – Ciba-Geigy (Switzerland)			✓	✓	28	✓			✓	✓	✓
Enteroviosulfa – Kimia Farma (Indonesia)	✓									✓	✓
Entrostop – Kalbe Farma (Indonesia)	✓					✓			✓	✓	✓
Himaform – Himalaya (Indonesia)	✓									✓	✓
Koniform – Konimex (Indonesia)	✓								✓	✓	
Libroform – Bintang Toedjoe (Indonesia)	✓					✓				✓	✓
Mexaform – Ciba-Geigy (Switzerland)				✓	28		✓				
Nifural – Pharos Chemie (Indonesia)	✓								✓		
Oletron – Bayer (W. Germany)	✓								✓		✓
Sulfa-Plus – Nellco (Indonesia)	✓									✓	✓
Viosulfon – Pharos Indonesia (Indonesia)	✓					✓			✓	✓	✓
MALAYSIA/SINGAPORE											
Entero-Vioform – Ciba-Geigy (Switzerland)	✓					✓				✓	✓
Entox – Wyeth (U.S.)	✓								✓		
Gastoquin – Cadila (India)	✓					✓					

TABLE 5 continued

	INDICATIONS						WARNINGS				
	Amebic Dysentery	Bacillary Dysentery	Diarrhea	"Traveler's Diarrhea," "Summer Diarrhea"	Enteritis & Enterocolitis	"Gastrointestinal Infections"	Maximum No. Days of Treatment	Sensitivity to Iodine, Hyperthyroidism	Caution in Kidney, Liver Disease	Optic, Other Nerve Damage	No Warnings
Kaoquin — Sigma (Australia)		✓	✓								✓
Mexaform — Ciba-Geigy (Switzerland)						✓					✓
Unidys Compound — Unichem (Thailand)			✓								✓
PHILIPPINES											
Entero-Vioform — Ciba-Geigy (Switzerland)	✓										✓
Mexaform — Ciba-Geigy (Switzerland)	✓	✓			✓						✓
Oletron — Bayer (W. Germany)	✓	✓	✓		✓						✓
CENTRAL AMERICA											
Clorpine — Endo (U.S.)	✓	✓	✓	✓			28	✓	✓	✓	
Entero-Vioformo — Ciba-Geigy (Switzerland)	✓	✓	✓		✓		28	✓	✓	✓	
Mexaformo — Ciba-Geigy (Switzerland)	✓	✓			✓		28	✓			
Nefurox — Richter (Italy)	✓	✓	✓		✓		7	✓			
Viotalidina — Carnot (Mexico)	✓	✓						✓		✓	

Note: All of these listed products except Entero-Vioform (o) and Enterosept contain clioquinol and other components.

products (28 days) in most areas and for Carnot's Viotalidina (7 days) in Central America.

The promotion of three clioquinol products in Central America is noteworthy. These are the only ones to warn physicians of the risk of nerve injury or optic atrophy, among the chief characteristics of SMON. It is not known whether this step represents a change in the marketing policies of the companies or in the editorial policy of the publishers or both.

Noteworthy, although for different reasons, are a number of products which combine clioquinol with one or more additional components. One of the most striking is Entomarcol, marketed in Nigeria by a Danish firm, Marcopharm Laboratories.[59] It is described to physicians as a "multifactor weapon against diarrhoeic conditions and intestinal infections of the most varied etiology." Its components:

— di-iodo-hydroxy-quinoline (a close relative of clioquinol)

— chloramphenicol

— a salt of streptomycin

— two sulfa-drugs

— furazolidine, another antidiarrheal agent

— pectin

— kaolin

— vitamin K_3

The composition of this somewhat unusual product was called to the attention of an internationally known Nigerian pharmacologist, widely respected for his tact, discretion, and restraint. He had only one comment: "Good God!"

Diphenoxylate

A relatively distant chemical relative of morphine, diphenoxylate is combined with atropine and marketed by Searle under the brand name of Lomotil as an antidiarrheal agent. Like other morphine-related substances, it has a pronounced constipating action, but its potential addicting properties are considered to be minimal. Administered to adults in normal dosages, it has few significant adverse reactions. In young children, however, the situation may be far different.

Clinical Background.   Authorities seem to agree that the incidence of side effects is low with recommended doses, but overdosage may lead to severe respiratory depression and coma. Caution is urged when the drug is given to patients with cirrhosis or other liver disease, or to those using sedatives and narcotics. Normal intestinal contractions may be totally stopped.

Young children, it is noted, are particularly susceptible to overdosage, and Lomotil should not be used for those under the age of two years.[60]

Promotion.   American physicians are warned in *PDR* that the drug should not be given to patients less than two years of age. The warning states:

LOMOTIL IS NOT AN INNOCUOUS DRUG AND DOSAGE RECOMMENDATIONS SHOULD BE STRICTLY ADHERED TO, ESPECIALLY IN CHILDREN.

Caution is recommended when liver disease is present, or the patient is taking sedatives or narcotic agents.

In Great Britain and Indonesia, dosage schedules are given for children as young as *one year.* In the Philippines and Central America, the Searle labeling suggests that Lomotil *may be given to infants as young as three months.*

PAIN AND FEVER FIGHTERS

From the mid-1880s until World War I, the German drug industry— an offshoot of Germany's gigantic chemical industry—came close to dominating the development and production of synthetic drugs throughout the world. Among the early products, most of them destined to earn enormous profits, were various agents that could control mild to moderate pain and reduce fever. These included antipyrine, antifebrin, or acetanilide, and phenacetin. (Aspirin would not appear until nearly 1900.) Antipyrine and antifebrin eventually had to be withdrawn because of their evident toxicity. Although phenacetin is still in use, it is facing increasing restrictions because of its serious or fatal action on the kidneys, and it may soon be banned in the United States. Some American companies have already withdrawn it.

Aminopyrine

One of the most important of these new agents was still another, known by such names as pyramidon, aminophenazone, and aminopyrine or amidopyrine. Even though aspirin later became the most widely used of all analgesic and antipyretic drugs, aminopyrine held a substantial part of the market.

Early in the twentieth century, it became obvious that aminopyrine was not an unmixed blessing. In some patients, it caused what is known as agranulocytosis, an acute condition marked by a pronounced lack of infection-battling white blood cells. There may also be infected ulcers in the mouth, throat, intestinal tract, and other mucous membranes, and involvement of the skin.[61] Totally unpredictable in its onset, this condition would often end in death.

By 1938, in the United States, this risk was considered to be so serious that the drug could not be sold over the counter without a physician's prescription. By 1970, a federal law required that each bottle must carry a label reading *This drug may cause fatal agranulocytosis.* A few years later, it was taken off the market. Other countries, notably Great Britain and Sweden, established similar restrictions. In a few instances, its cautious use was permitted to control the fever in patients dying from inoperable cancer or other diseases that could not be helped by any other means.

Spokesmen for many of the major companies involved—mainly Hoechst, Boehringer Mannheim, and Ravensberg in Germany, Polfa in Poland, and Ciba-Geigy and Sandoz in Switzerland—were disappointed by such developments. They had, in fact, long pooh-poohed the dangers of aminopyrine.

"Some of the debate was rather heated," recalls British-trained Leader Stirling, for many years Minister of Health in Tanzania. He told us this:

> I remember the time—it must have been in the middle or late 1930s—I went back to visit my old medical school in England. There was a conference on aminopyrine, and the drug came in for some British criticism. In the audience was a representative of one of the German firms that was

making the drug. He took as much of this criticism as he could and then leaped to his feet. "You must understand," he announced, "that amino-pyrine is a safe drug! The German Reich does not produce dangerous drugs! Aminopyrine is safe!" And then, stretching his arm toward the ceiling, he called out, "Heil Hitler!"[62]

By and large, German and Swiss company representatives insisted, agranulocytosis was a British or an American—or possibly a Swedish—disease. It did not occur in Africa, or in Asia, or anywhere in South America.

"In Korea," one expert says, "the drug representative actually told our people in the Ministry of Health that aminopyrine is without any danger."[63] In one African country, a pediatrician says, there was "a hush-hush campaign to convince doctors that aminopyrine was far safer than aspirin for children." In Kenya, physicians were told that the pre-ferred drug for pain-control was not aspirin but aminopyrine, prefer-ably administered by injection.

Finally, to the visible anguish of particularly Ciba-Geigy in Switzer-land and Hoechst in Germany, many countries began to have the drug taken off the market. To Swiss Ciba-Geigy, perhaps the unkindest cut came when the drug was withdrawn in Switzerland. Curiously, these steps came not as a recognition of the dangers of agranulocytosis but because new evidence appeared to suggest that aminopyrine, either by itself or in combination with the nitrites in some foods, might cause cancer.

Early in 1977, Ciba-Geigy and Sandoz announced that its pain and fever remedies containing aminopyrine would be removed from the market or reformulated by the end of that year. Hoechst announced it would take similar steps, except possibly in the case of Spain. Drug experts were relieved. For whatever the reason, they assumed, the cor-rect action would be taken promptly. Then came the case of C.B.

In the summer of 1979, C.B. was a 27-year-old English schoolteacher working in the East African country of Mozambique. She developed a slight fever, along with a sore throat and aches in her arms, legs, and back. She treated herself with some tablets of Ciba's Cibalgin, which she had purchased at a local pharmacy. After four days, however, the fever had become worse. Ulcers were forming on her lips, and there was tooth pain, colicky pain in her abdomen, and vomiting. Her temperature had soared to 104° F., and her white blood count was dropping alarmingly.
    She was hospitalized first in Mozambique, where physicians tried to

control what seemed to be some baffling infection. In spite of the treatment, more ulcers broke out on the roof of her mouth and lower lip, and red streaks and nodules appeared on her limbs and trunk.

Still suffering from the fever, the ulcers, and a necrosis which eventually exposed both her upper and lower jawbones, she was flown to the Reitfontein Hospital in Johannesburg. Finally, after six weeks of hospital treatment, the acute state was brought under control.[64]

"She came very close to dying," British physician John Yudkin said afterwards. "Her weight had dropped from 110 pounds to 70. She had to be given substantial oral surgery and dental care. But she survived."[65]

There are several intriguing points involved in the case of C.B. "If she had been some poor Mozambican peasant woman, she would not have had the investigations that made it possible to diagnose her condition. It's possible that many people throughout the Third World die every day from drug-induced illness that is put down as malaria or other disease," says Yudkin.

But C.B. was not some unknown native woman. One of her friends and near neighbors was Paul Epstein, an American physician working in Africa as a volunteer. Another was a British magazine writer. They called upon Yudkin, who himself had worked in neighboring Tanzania and who joined with Epstein in sending the case report to *Lancet*.

One oddity concerned how Cibalgin, which presumably had been removed from the market by the end of 1977, could have been purchased in Africa *in 1979*. Another involved the discovery, made by C.B. herself, that Ciba's Cibalgin—containing the original aminopyrine formulation—was available in a modern pharmacy in Portugal *in the summer of 1980*.

Ciba's defense was simple: no country had enacted a law requiring the company to go through each pharmacy and remove Cibalgin from its shelves.

Clinical Background.   As early as 1970, Goodman and Gilman warned physicians that aminopyrine can cause severe and often fatal agranulocytosis, and its "clinical use has been sharply curtailed."[66] In 1975, British physicians were told by *Martindale:* "The risk of agranulocytosis in patients taking aminopyrine is sufficiently great to render this drug unsuitable for use."[67] The 1977 edition of *AMA Drug Evaluations* in the United States stated (p. 341) that the use of the drug "has become obsolete in this country"; it was dropped completely from the 1980 edition.

Promotion.   No product containing aminopyrine is mentioned in *PDR* or *MIMS UK.* The reference books for Africa, Malaysia/Singapore, and the Philippines show that the aminopyrine has been replaced by closely related derivatives. Whether these are safer than aminopyrine is not clear.

Listed in the book for Indonesia are Konimex's Piralgin, Dupa's Xylomidon, and Phapros's Pehazon. All contain aminopyrine. None carries a warning against agranulocytosis.

The reference work for Central America includes descriptions of Ciba-Geigy's Espasma-Cibalgina and the products of two Spanish firms, Liade's Hemicraneal and Lacer's Meloka. No specific warnings about agranulocytosis are given for the first two, and no warning of any kind is presented for the third.

Dipyrone

As physicians, especially in the United States and Great Britain, became increasingly aware of the risk of severe or lethal blood damage with aminopyrine, they turned instead to another agent, called dipyrone. Some manufacturers also marketed the latter under such names as metamizol, noramidopyrine, sulpyrine, and methampyrone.

The reasons for this multiplicity of names are not clear. There is at least the possibility that they merely confused some physicians, leading them to believe that dipyrone and the now-feared aminopyrine were quite different. Dipyrone is, in fact, a close chemical relative of aminopyrine. It, too, can cause serious or fatal agranulocytosis.

Clinical Background.   In the United Kingdom, the toxic effects of dipyrone are described simply with this phrase, "as for amidopyrine." According to *Martindale,* its use "is justified only in serious or life-threatening situations where no alternative antipyretic is available or suitable" (p. 191).

American physicians were advised in the 1973 edition of *AMA Drug Evaluations* that dipyrone was already being used—and used unwisely—to replace aminopyrine.

There is evidence that dipyrone, a derivative of aminopyrine that shares its potential for toxicity, unfortunately is still being misused. This is probably because it is available in injectable form and because physicians do not recognize its similarity to aminopyrine since it is marketed under various trademarks. . . . Its only justifiable use is as a last resort to reduce fever when safer measures have failed. . . . Because dipyrone may produce fatal agranulocytosis and other blood dyscrasias, its use as a general analgesic, antiarthritic, or routine antipyretic cannot be condoned. (Pp. 262, 267)

In the 1977 edition of the same publication, it was stated (p. 341) that the drug had become obsolete in the United States. In the 1980 edition, it was not even listed.

Promotion. In the latest editions of *PDR* in the United States and *MIMS* in the United Kingdom, dipyrone products are not included. But, as is shown in Table 6, they are obviously being widely used or at least promoted in developing countries. In general, they are recommended for all kinds of pain from headache, rheumatic and arthritic pain, lumbago, and neuralgia to toothache and menstrual discomfort. Some are advocated to relieve the inflammation of arthritis.

In this table, attention is focused primarily on the warnings against agranulocytosis, although some product labeling mentions "sensitivity," a word which may or may not indicate a hypersensitivity involved in causing blood damage.

As is the case with other drugs, there is no visible consistency in the labeling of dipyrone products. For the American Winthrop group, including Sterling-Winthrop and Winthrop-Stearns, Germany's E. Merck and Hoechst, and Japan's Tanabe, essentially the same products carry agranulocytosis warnings in some Third World countries but not in others.

There is no apparent relation to any government policies within the countries. Thus some multinational company products and some domestic company products carry such warnings in Indonesia, while the products marketed by other multinational and domestic companies do not. Warnings against agranulocytosis are given in Africa for Algopyrone, produced by Medimpex of Hungary, but not for Pyralgin, marketed by Polfa of Poland. It is noteworthy that *all* the dipyrone products listed here for the Philippines are labeled to caution physicians of the risk of

	WARNINGS		
TABLE 6 **DIPYRONE** Products: Warnings	Warning of Agranulocytosis	Warning of Fatal Agranulocytosis	No Agranulocytosis Warning
UNITED STATES None Listed			
UNITED KINGDOM None Listed			
AFRICA[a]			
Abalgine — Adelco (Greece)	✔		
Algopyrone — Medimpex (Hungary)	✔		
Conmel — Winthrop (U.S.)	✔		
Dispalgine — Adelco (Greece)	✔		
Dolo-Neurobion — E. Merck (W. Germany)	✔		
Lagalgin — Lagap (Switzerland)	✔		
Natralgin — Chropi (Greece)			✔
Pyralgin — Polfa (Poland)			✔
INDONESIA[a]			
Beserol — Sterling-Winthrop (U.S.)			✔
Bestopyron — Tanabe-Abadi (Japan)	✔		
Bonpyrin — Takeda (Japan)	#		
Cetalgin — Soho (Indonesia)	#		
Conmel — Sterling-Winthrop (U.S.)			✔
Cosadon — Phapros (Indonesia)			✔
Deparon — Westmont (Philippines)	✔		
Dia-Fastalgin — Pharos (Indonesia)	✔		
Dolo Neurobion — E. Merck (W. Germany)	✔		
Dolo Scanneuron — Scanchemie (Indonesia)	✔		
Fastalgin — Pharos (Indonesia)	✔		
Hifluton — Himalaya (Indonesia)			✔
Himagen — Himalaya (Indonesia)			✔
Meta Bioneuron — Phapros (Indonesia)	✔		

TABLE 6 continued

	Warning of Agranulocytosis	Warning of Fatal Agranulocytosis	No Agranulocytosis Warning
	WARNINGS		
Metaneuron — Phapros (Indonesia)			✔
Neo-Protal — Apex (Indonesia)	#		
Neuralgin — Kalbe Farma (Indonesia)			✔
Neurobat A — Interbat (Indonesia)			✔
Neuro-Novalgin — Hoechst (W. Germany)	✔		
Novalgin — Hoechst (W. Germany)	✔		
Piralgin F — Konimex (Indonesia)			✔
Pyronal — Tanabe-Abadi (Japan)			✔
Ronalgin — Dexa (Indonesia)			✔
Supranal — Dexa (Indonesia)			✔
Unagen with AMB — United American (Philippines)	✔		
Xylomidon — Dupa (Indonesia)			✔
MALAYSIA/SINGAPORE[a]			
Bonpyrin — Takeda (Japan)			✔
Conmel — Winthrop-Sterling (U.S.)			✔
Deparon — Westmont (Philippines)	✔		
Dolo-Adamon — Asta-Werke (W. Germany)	✔		
Dolo-Neurobion — E. Merck (W. Germany)			✔
Novalgin — Hoechst (W. Germany)			✔
PHILIPPINES[a]			
Anaretic — Rafgers (Philippines)	✔		
Bagaron — Roche (Switzerland)[b]	✔	✔	
Beserol — Winthrop-Stearns (U.S.)	✔		
Bipyrine — Pascual/Pharex (Philippines)	✔		
Cenafeb — Biochemica (Philippines)	✔	✔	
Conmel — Winthrop-Stearns (U.S.)	✔		
Dolo-Neurobion — E. Merck (W. Germany)	✔		
Dovran — Uni-Med/Doctors Pharm (Philippines)	✔		
Dyrone — Medicalex/Doctors Pharm (Philippines)	✔		
Fivepyron — Five-Med Labs. (Philippines)	✔		

TABLE 6 continued	WARNINGS		
	Warning of Agranulocytosis	Warning of Fatal Agranulocytosis	No Agranulocytosis Warning
Gardan — Winthrop-Stearns (U.S.)	✓		
Gifaril — Wander (Switzerland)	✓	✓	
Melubrin — Hoechst (W. Germany)	✓	✓	
Novaldin — Winthrop-Stearns (U.S.)	✓		
Pacipyrine — Siemsgluss/Pacific Pharm. (W. Germany/Philippines)	✓	✓	
Piril — Doctors Pharm./Unicor (Philippines)	✓		
Pyran — Hizon (Philippines)	✓	✓	
Unagen — United American (Philippines)	✓		
CENTRAL AMERICA[a]			
Conmel — Winthrop (U.S.)	#		
Sinalgex — Solka (Nicaragua)			✓
Tophalgin-B15 — Rarpe (Nicaragua)			✓

Note: # = Nonspecific "sensitivity" warning.
[a] Combinations with antispasmodics not included.
[b] Not produced since 1979.

agranulocytosis. Some product labeling warns that the agranulocytosis may be fatal.

ANABOLIC HORMONES: THE "TISSUE BUILDERS"

The anabolic hormones, most of them weak versions of male sex hormones, were synthesized and introduced into medicine as agents to speed the transformation of foodstuffs into body tissues. They were originally promoted—and some still are—as drugs that could stimulate appetite, step up body weight, strengthen bones, increase athletic ability, control a variety of emaciating diseases, and aid in recovery from surgery, infections, burns, fractures, and severe traumatic injuries.

Few of these proposed applications have survived scientific study. Currently, on the basis of objective evidence, the anabolic hormones are accepted mainly for the control of certain kinds of anemia and some forms of inoperable breast cancer, and perhaps for prevention or treatment of osteoporosis, or bone-softening, which strikes many postmenopausal women and senile patients.

Unfortunately, these substances are only weak male sex hormones, but nonetheless they act like male sex hormones. Given in large amounts, they may cause baldness, deepening of the voice, hirsutism, and menstrual irregularities in women. In young children, they can cause too early closure of epiphyses in the bones and result in stunted growth. In young boys, they can lead to precocious sexual development. In young girls, they can produce enlargement of the clitoris or the development of a false penis. Some manufacturers, in the past, have neglected to warn physicians of these masculinizing changes,[68] or the physicians failed to heed the warning.

A few years ago, a Sri Lanka physician trained at the University of Manchester in England gave this account to British Broadcasting Corporation reporters:

> In Manchester, we demonstrated a case of a little baby, an eight-months-old girl, with an enormous pseudo-penis . . . this child had been given one of those anabolic steroids . . . you couldn't make out whether the child was a girl or a boy. . . . The treatment was discussed . . . we will remove this objectionable penis in a girl. . . . At the end, one of the professors said, "Well, we haven't mentioned prevention. . . . The prevention is, I think, we should cut off the real penis of the doctor who prescribed this."[69]

Clinical Background. There seems to be substantial evidence that the anabolic hormones, in large doses, can aid in the treatment of such recalcitrant forms of anemia as aplastic anemia and that associated with kidney failure, and help control metastatic cancer of the breast in some patients.[70] In the treatment of bone-softening, an expert panel of the National Academy of Sciences/National Research Council concluded that these drugs are "probably" effective. Drug experts have emphasized that the drugs can help transform food into body protein *only* if the patient is getting enough food, particularly enough protein and total calories.[71]

"The use of anabolic steroids to improve athletic performance is unanimously condemned," says *AMA Drug Evaluations*. "Not only is this a trivial indication, but experimental evidence suggests that steroids do not significantly increase muscle size or strength in healthy young men who are already in good physical condition."[72] There is, moreover, the risk that large doses given to athletes will cause liver damage and interference with testicular function.

Promotion. As recently as 1980, various anabolic hormone products were being advocated for such applications as these:

— In Africa, the Greek company Adelco was promoting Anaboline to overcome loss of weight.

— In Africa, the German firm Schering AG was promoting its Dacomid for cirrhosis of the liver and chronic hepatitis, its Fortabol for "poor general health," and its Primobolan Depot for "wasting diseases." The last product was also being recommended in Latin America to aid malnourished children.

— In Africa, the French firm Roussel was promoting its Glosso-Sterandryl for treatment of debility and emaciation.

— In Africa, the Hungarian group Medimpex was recommending its Nerobol for senility and muscular dystrophy.

— In Indonesia, the Indonesian company Dupa was promoting its Anabolene for appetite improvement, pernicious anemia, lack of energy, and poor weight gain.

— In Indonesia, the Swiss firm Ciba-Geigy was promoting its Dianavit for reduced resistance to infection, tiredness, and debility.

— In Indonesia, Malaysia, and Singapore, Organon of the Netherlands was recommending its Fertabolin for poor appetite, low weight gain, lack of energy, lack of stamina, and listlessness.

In the Third World countries concerned here, it is not clear how much of the "loss of weight," "poor general health," "wasting diseases," "child malnourishment," "debility," "emaciation," "lack of energy," "poor weight gain," "tiredness," "lack of stamina," and "listlessness" can be attributed to a need for hormone therapy and how much simply to starvation.

Here particular consideration is given to the promotion and labeling of three widely used anabolic hormones: Winstrol, a form of stanozolol marketed by the U.S. firm Winthrop or, in Great Britain, as Stromba, marketed by its affiliate Sterling Research Laboratories; Durabolin, a form of nandrolone phenpropionate marketed by Organon; and Diana-bol, a form of methandrostenolone marketed by Ciba-Geigy.

In the case of Winstrol or Stromba, the indications for use are gener-ally the same in the United States, the Philippines, and Central Ameri-ca, covering stimulation of protein synthesis, the control of osteoporosis ("probably" effective in the United States), the treatment of aplastic anemia, and an aid in convalescence or debilitating disease. It is recom-mended in the United Kingdom and Africa only for osteoporosis and debilitating disease, and in Malaysia/Singapore only as an aid in pro-tein synthesis.

In the care of patients with postmenopausal or senile osteoporosis, American physicians are told that the drug may be effective as an ad-junct but not as primary therapy. "Equal or greater consideration should be given to diet, calcium balance, physiotherapy, and good gener-al health-promoting measures."

For Durabolin, the uses promoted in the United States, the Philip-pines, and Central America are similar, and include its application in the control of metastatic breast cancer. Fewer specific indications are listed in Great Britain, Indonesia, and Malaysia/Singapore.

Dianabol is recommended only for the treatment of osteoporosis in the United States, but is recommended for use in convalescence and in the promotion of growth and weight increase in Great Britain, Africa, and Indonesia.

The major warnings and contraindications listed for these three prod-ucts are shown in Table 7.

The warnings for Winstrol presented in the United States and in Central America are virtually the same. In both areas, physicians are advised that the drug should not be used in any attempt to enhance athletic ability. The possible masculinization of young girls is not men-tioned in Great Britain, Malaysia/Singapore, or the Philippines, and the risk of stunted growth is not listed in Africa, Malaysia/Singapore, or the Philippines.

In the case of Durabolin, again the warnings given in the United States and Central America are closely alike. The promotion in the United Kingdom, Indonesia, Malaysia/Singapore, and the Philippines

TABLE 7

ANABOLIC HORMONES:
Warnings

	WARNINGS								
	No Use to Enhance Athletic Ability	Caution in Heart, Kidney, Liver Disease	Caution in Male Breast, Prostate Cancer	Caution in Female Breast Cancer	Caution in Pregnancy	Caution in Children	Growth Stunting in Children	Masculinization of Girls, Women	Menstrual Irregularities
STANOZOLOL PRODUCTS									
UNITED STATES									
Winstrol – Winthrop (U.S.)	✓	✓	✓	✓	✓	✓	✓	✓	✓
UNITED KINGDOM									
Stromba – Sterling Research Labs. (U.S.)		✓	✓	✓	✓	✓	✓		
AFRICA									
Winstrol – Winthrop (U.S.)		✓	✓	✓	✓			✓	
MALAYSIA/SINGAPORE									
Winstrol – Winthrop (U.S.)		✓	✓	✓	✓				
PHILIPPINES									
Winstrol – Winthrop (U.S.)		✓	✓	✓	✓			✓	
CENTRAL AMERICA									
Winstrol – Winthrop (U.S.)	✓	✓	✓	✓	✓	✓	✓	✓	✓

TABLE 7 continued

NANDROLONE PRODUCTS	No Use to Enhance Athletic Ability	Caution in Heart, Kidney, Liver Disease	Caution in Male Breast, Prostate Cancer	Caution in Female Breast Cancer	Caution in Pregnancy	Caution in Children	Growth Stunting in Children	Masculinization of Girls, Women	Menstrual Irregularities
UNITED STATES									
Durabolin—Organon (Netherlands)	✓	✓	✓		✓	✓	✓	✓	✓
UNITED KINGDOM									
Durabolin—Organon (Netherlands)			✓		✓				
INDONESIA									
Durabolin—Organon (Netherlands)			✓		✓				
MALAYSIA/SINGAPORE									
Durabolin—Organon (Netherlands)			✓		✓				
PHILIPPINES									
Durabolin—Organon (Netherlands)			✓		✓				
CENTRAL AMERICA									
Durabolin—Organon (Netherlands)			✓		✓	✓	✓	✓	

TABLE 7 continued

METHANDROSTENOLONE PRODUCTS	WARNINGS								
	No Use to Enhance Athletic Ability	Caution in Heart, Kidney, Liver Disease	Caution in Male Breast, Prostate Cancer	Caution in Female Breast Cancer	Caution in Pregnancy	Caution in Children	Growth Stunting in Children	Masculinization of Girls, Women	Menstrual Irregularities
UNITED STATES									
Dianabol – Ciba-Geigy (Switzerland)	✓	✓	✓	✓	✓	✓	✓	✓	✓
UNITED KINGDOM									
Dianabol – Ciba-Geigy (Switzerland)[a]		✓	✓		✓				
AFRICA									
Dianabol – Ciba-Geigy (Switzerland)[a]									
INDONESIA									
Dianabol – Ciba-Geigy (Switzerland)									

[a] Only warning: limit period of continuous treatment.

Note: In March 1982, because of problems in controlling irrational use, Ciba-Geigy ordered that Dianabol be taken off the market worldwide, with all stocks to be destroyed.

does not contain warnings about growth-stunting, the possible masculinization of girls or women, or the development of menstrual irregularities.

For Dianabol, a long list of warnings is given in the United States,
but only a few are presented for Indonesia. In Great Britain and Africa,
physicians are urged only to administer the drug for limited periods.
(Since 1978 and until at least 1980, Ciba-Geigy has repeatedly requested the publisher of *MIMS Africa* to include a warning about the risk of
masculinization in its description of Dianabol, but no change has yet
been made.)[73] Except for the United States labeling, specific warnings
about growth-stunting and masculinization are generally missing.

TONICS: SOME OF THIS, SOME OF THAT

High on the list of moneymaking drug products in many countries, rich
or poor, industrialized or underdeveloped alike, are combinations of
various ingredients which can be administered in a single pill. In the
United States, Great Britain, and other developed nations, the most
popular of these are combinations of multivitamins, or multivitamins
plus multiminerals, or multivitamins plus multiminerals plus amino
acids. Originally lauded as beneficial for most of the ills of man and
beast—especially those of aging men and aging beasts—most of these
concoctions, fortunately, can do little or no harm, except possibly to the
pocketbooks of those who neither need nor can afford them.

Nutrition experts have long been able to prove that most individuals
on a normal diet have no need for vitamin supplements. Much of the
additional vitamin intake is simply excreted through the kidneys, and
accordingly America is said to have probably the most nutritious sewage
in the world.

In most developed countries, the advertising and the promotion of
major vitamin and mineral supplements is now being kept within reasonable bounds. This is particularly true of the United States, where the
Food and Drug Administration and the Federal Trade Commission
have had to rap the knuckles of companies such as the makers of Geritol
and their advertising agencies for making public claims that were without acceptable scientific support.

The situation in many Third World countries is different. There,
claims for the values of vitamins and minerals may grossly exceed what

can be supported with scientific evidence. In the Third World, such advertising—whether to physicians or to the public—is especially shocking. The problem for the poor people of the Third World—which means most of the people—is not a shortage of vitamins, it is a shortage of food.

In addition, ingenious drug companies—many of them relatively small firms—have gone far beyond vitamins and minerals in their sales campaigns for the Third World. They have created concoctions and promotional campaigns for them which, as one drug expert put it, would have made purveyors of snake oil turn green with envy. Among them are the following:

— In Indonesia: Kimla Farma's Padibu, composed of a male sex hormone, strychnine, arsenic, caffeine, and yohimbine. (Yohimbine, a substance derived from a West African tree, has been occasionally touted as an aphrodisiac, but there is no convincing evidence to support this or any other use.)[74]

— In Indonesia: Pharos Chemie's Potentol, containing a male sex hormone, royal bee jelly, ginseng, vitamin B complex plus vitamins A, C, D, E, and K3, inositol, methionine, biotin, glutaminic acid, lecithin, rutin, lysine, minerals, sulphur, and safflower oil.

— In Indonesia: Samphindo's Vixtron-G, recommended for the treatment of underdeveloped testes or ovaries, impotence, the "menopausal syndrome," and the "male climacteric." It contains a male sex hormone, a female sex hormone, ginseng, vitamins A, B1, B2, B12, E, and K, niacinamide, pantothenate, rutin, methionine, choline, and inositol.

— In the Philippines: Aminobrain, marketed by the Philippine firm Nordia, containing ginseng, royal bee jelly, procaine, vitamins C and E, lysine, nicotinamide, and elemental iron. Included in the labeling is the following: "Increases the general intellectual capacities through improved memory and concentration, restores youthful stamina, enhances sexual fulfillment through increased libido, reduces risk of cardiovascular complications by lowering the cholesterol and lipid contents of the blood and preventing formation of blood clots, helps check circulatory disturbances, stimulates appetite and supplements restrictive diet."

— In the Philippines: Biontabol, marketed by the German firm of E. Merck, including bromelains, pyritinol, and vitamins A, B6, and E. It is advocated in cases of decreased physical and intellectual function, and to alleviate weakness, overwork, mental strain, exhaustion, weight loss, and digestive trouble. (Bromelains are protein-splitting enzymes which have been vigorously promoted for use in a variety of inflammatory states. Their value when administered by mouth remains to be established.)[75]

— In the Philippines and also in Central America: Geriatric Pharmaton, marketed by Pharmaton of Switzerland. Including ginseng, substance H3, vitamins, minerals, and lipotropics, it is said to be indicated for "prevention and relief of complaints due to old age, improvement of memory, relief from depressions, inducement of deeper and more relaxed sleep, increase of mental and physical efficiency."

— In the Philippines: Medichem's Mysgen, composed of a male sex hormone, yohimbine, strychnine, ginseng, vitamin E, and nicotinate. The labeling states: "To improve physical and mental work capacity and prolong endurance in athletic activities, promote a happy disposition, intensify male image or profile, and enhance sexual fulfillment. . . . Not recommended for use in women."

— In Central America: Scanviril, marketed by Scanpharm of Denmark, containing a male sex hormone, yohimbine, nicotinic acid, and vitamins B1, B6, and E. It is recommended for the treatment of "masculine impotence, the male climacteric, and disturbances of fertility."

It should be noted that none of the combination products mentioned here, nor few if any others like them, are listed in *Physicians' Desk Reference* in the United States, *MIMS UK* in Great Britain, or, for that matter, in *MIMS Africa*.

A drug company official put the matter in these words. "Don't knock those combinations. They make very large profits. They sell, so they can't be all bad." Or, to paraphrase a onetime General Motors leader, "If it's good for the drug industry, it's good for society."

Although the use of many tonics and similar preparations may be scientifically and economically irrational, especially in the poorer countries, their popularity can scarcely be questioned. This is particularly true in Moslem countries of the Third World, where the use of alcoholic beverages is forbidden. Some of these tonics contain alcohol in concentrations up to 40 proof.

"THE PILL"

Controversy has never been a stranger to the consideration of oral contraceptives. Since the first clinical studies conducted in Puerto Rico during the late 1950s, with the discovery there of several "inexplicable deaths," the use and promotion of these drugs have remained at the center of clinical, sociological, ethical, religious, and even political dispute.[76] The results of statistical studies have been challenged unto the nth decimal point. It has been claimed that unpleasant or even dangerous side effects occur more frequently with use of The Pill than in a normal pregnancy, or less frequently, or at about the same rate. The dangers of The Pill have been dismissed as no greater than those associated with driving on a highway, although the relevance of such a comparison remains unclear.

In some industrialized countries, packets of oral contraceptives may be handed to patients along with a so-called patient package insert, designed to give instructions on appropriate use of the products and the possibility of untoward effects. On the one hand, these leaflets have been praised as giving each patient a chance to make an informed choice; on the basis of what she reads—along with what she may be told by her physician or pharmacist—she may make an informed decision on whether or not to take the drug. On ·the other hand, it has been denounced as interfering with the seemingly sacred "doctor-patient relationship."

In the United States, over the vociferous opposition of organized medical groups, the distribution of patient package inserts on The Pill has been required by FDA since 1970. Since 1970, there appears to be no evidence that doctor-patient relationships have grown visibly better or worse.

Clinical Background. There is apparently no doubt that oral contraceptives, providing they are taken faithfully on the appropriate schedule, can give remarkably effective control of conception.[77] There is substantially less agreement on their value in the control of premenstrual tension, dysmenorrhea or menstrual pain, problems of the menopause, functional or endocrine infertility, and other conditions.[78]

There is likewise substantial agreement that the various oral contraceptive products can cause reactions ranging from the trivial or unimportant to serious or even life-threatening. Some of the common but less serious reactions may be only temporary, disappearing after the first two or three months of use. Where more important reactions are concerned, experts generally indicate that these are relatively infrequent. They may involve blood-vessel inflammation and the formation of blood clots that can lodge in the lungs, heart, or brain. In the last few years, however, the statistical significance of the early studies linking such clots with The Pill has been questioned by some workers who believe that contraceptives are less hazardous than such factors as cigarette smoking.[79] In some patients, the oral contraceptives can influence preexisting cancer of the breast, uterus, or other sexual organs. Rarely, there may be serious or life-threatening changes in the liver.[80]

The risk of serious adverse reactions caused by oral contraceptive products is apparently small, involving perhaps scores to possibly several hundred per one million users a year. Nevertheless, these hazards may not be safely ignored. Any potential injury concerning drugs used by tens of millions of presumably healthy women each year warrants attention. Experts stress that The Pill should not be used, or should be used only with caution, by women with any record of blood-vessel disease, known or even suspected hormone-dependent cancer, impaired liver function, emotional disorder, epilepsy, asthma, migraine, or impaired heart or kidney function. Not all experts are in agreement on all these contraindications. Many authorities recommend that women taking The Pill should undergo a regular breast and pelvic examination.

These precautions apply to every oral contraceptive now on the world market. Although there are many of these products available in advanced and developing countries, essentially all of them are combinations of only about half a dozen different sex-hormone derivatives, or a single hormone used alone.

Promotion. As is shown in Table 8, identical indications and warnings are presented for all of the roughly 40 products listed for the United States, for the 30 listed for Great Britain, and for 30 of the 32

TABLE 8

ORAL CONTRACEPTIVES:
Indications and Warnings

	INDICATIONS					WARNINGS				
	Contraception	Regularization of Menstrual Cycle	Premenstrual Tension	Menstrual Pain	Other Uses[a]	Thromboembolic Phenomena[b]	Hormone-dependent Tumor	Impaired Liver Function	Other Warnings[c]	No Warnings
UNITED STATES All oral contraceptive products	✓				✓	✓	✓	✓	✓	
UNITED KINGDOM All oral contraceptive products	✓					✓	✓	✓	✓	
AFRICA										
Bisecurin – Medimpex (Hungary)	✓					✓	✓	✓	✓	
Eugynon ED – Schering AG (W. Germany)	✓			✓		✓	✓	✓	✓	
All other oral contraceptive products	✓	✓		✓	✓	✓	✓	✓	✓	
INDONESIA										
Agestin ED – Kalbe Farma (Indonesia)	✓	✓		✓	✓	✓	✓	✓	✓	
Eugynon ED – Schering AG (W. Germany)	✓									✓
Lyndiol – Organon (Netherlands)	✓									✓
Microgynon – Schering AG (W. Germany)	✓	✓		✓	✓	✓	✓	✓	✓	
Neogynon – Schering AG (W. Germany)	✓	✓		✓	✓	✓	✓	✓	✓	

TABLE 8 continued

	INDICATIONS					WARNINGS				
	Contraception	Regularization of Menstrual Cycle	Premenstrual Tension	Menstrual Pain	Other Uses[a]	Thromboembolic Phenomena[b]	Hormone-dependent Tumor	Impaired Liver Function	Other Warnings[c]	No Warnings
Nordette — Wyeth (U.S.)	✓				✓	✓	✓	✓	✓	
Nordiol — Wyeth (U.S.)	✓					✓	✓	✓	✓	
Ovostat — Organon (Netherlands)	✓								✓	
Ovulen — Searle (U.S.)	✓									
Restovar — Organon (Netherlands)	✓					✓				✓
MALAYSIA/SINGAPORE										
Anovlar — Schering AG (W. Germany)	✓			✓	✓					✓
Brevinor — Syntex (Panama)	✓									✓
Conovid-E — Searle (U.S.)	✓						✓			
Duoluton — Schering AG (W. Germany)	✓									✓
Eugynon — Schering AG (W. Germany)	✓	✓		✓	✓					✓
Gynovlar — Schering AG (W. Germany)	✓	✓		✓	✓					✓
Lyndiol — Organon (Netherlands)	✓			✓	✓					
Microgynon — Schering AG (W. Germany)	✓						✓	✓	✓	
Microlut — Schering AG (W. Germany)	✓					✓	✓	✓	✓	
Ministat — Organon (Netherlands)	✓							✓		✓

TABLE 8 continued

	INDICATIONS					WARNINGS				
	Contraception	Regularization of Menstrual Cycle	Premenstrual Tension	Menstrual Pain	Other Uses[a]	Thromboembolic Phenomena[b]	Hormone-dependent Tumor	Impaired Liver Function	Other Warnings[c]	No Warnings
Neogynon – Schering AG (W. Germany)	✓	✓		✓	✓	✓		✓	✓	
Noracyclin – Ciba-Geigy (Switzerland)	✓					✓	✓	✓	✓	
Nordette – Wyeth (U.S.)	✓					✓	✓	✓		✓
Nordiol – Wyeth (U.S.)	✓					✓		✓	✓	
Noriday – Syntex (Panama)	✓						✓	✓		✓
Norinyl – Syntex (Panama)	✓						✓	✓		✓
Noristerat – Schering AG (W. Germany)	✓		✓	✓	✓					✓
Ovostat – Organon (Netherlands)	✓									
Ovral – Wyeth (U.S.)	✓					✓		✓	✓	
Ovulen – Searle (U.S.)	✓						✓	✓	✓	
Postinor – Gedeon Richter (Hungary)	✓									
Rigevidon – Gedeon Richter (Hungary)	✓									
PHILIPPINES										
Anovlar – Schering AG (W. Germany)	✓	✓			✓	✓	✓	✓	✓	
Femenal – Wyeth (U.S.)	✓						✓		✓	
Lyndiol – Organon (Netherlands)	✓		✓	✓	✓					

TABLE 8 continued

	INDICATIONS					WARNINGS				
	Contraception	Regularization of Menstrual Cycle	Premenstrual Tension	Menstrual Pain	Other Uses[a]	Thromboembolic Phenomena[b]	Hormone-dependent Tumor	Impaired Liver Function	Other Warnings[c]	No Warnings
Micropil – Pascual/Pharex (Philippines)	✓	✓		✓	✓	✓	✓	✓	✓	
Minovlar – Schering AG (W. Germany)	✓	✓			✓	✓	✓	✓	✓	
Nordiol – Wyeth (U.S.)	✓								✓	✓
Ovostat – Organon (Netherlands)	✓	✓								
Ovulen – Searle (U.S.)	✓	✓	✓	✓	✓	✓		✓	✓	
Ovysmen – Ortho (U.S.)	✓					✓				
CENTRAL AMERICA										
Anovlar – Schering AG (W. Germany)	d	✓			✓	✓	✓	✓	✓	
Demilen – Searle (U.S.)	✓	✓		✓	✓	✓	✓	✓	✓	
Denoval – Wyeth (U.S.)	✓			✓		✓	✓	✓	✓	
Duoluton – Schering AG (W. Germany)	✓					✓	✓	✓	✓	
Enavid – Searle (U.S.)	d		✓			✓	✓	✓	✓	
Eugynon – Schering AG (W. Germany)	d					✓	✓	✓	✓	
Gynovlar – Schering AG (W. Germany)	e					✓	✓	✓	✓	
Lindiol – Organon (Netherlands)	d					✓	✓	✓	✓	
Mesovul – Ufarmex (Mexico)	d					✓	✓	✓	✓	
Microgynon – Schering AG (W. Germany)	d					✓	✓	✓	✓	

TABLE 8 continued

	INDICATIONS					WARNINGS				
	Contraception	Regularization of Menstrual Cycle	Premenstrual Tension	Menstrual Pain	Other Uses[a]	Thromboembolic Phenomena[b]	Hormone-dependent Tumor	Impaired Liver Function	Other Warnings[c]	No Warnings
Microlut – Schering AG (W. Germany)	✓					✓	✓	✓	✓	
Neogynon – Schering AG (W. Germany)	d					✓	✓	✓	✓	
Nordette – Wyeth (U.S.)	✓					✓	✓	✓	✓	
Norinyl – Syntex (Panama)	e					✓	✓	✓	✓	
Norlestrin – Parke-Davis (U.S.)	e	✓	✓	✓	✓	✓	✓	✓	✓	
Ortho-Novum – Ortho (U.S.)	e					✓	✓	✓	✓	
Ovostat – Organon (Netherlands)	✓					✓	✓	✓	✓	
Ovral – Wyeth (U.S.)	e					✓	✓	✓	✓	
Ovulen – Searle (U.S.)	✓					✓	✓	✓	✓	
Planocol – Europharma (Panama)	✓		✓	✓	✓					✓
Primovlar – Schering AG (W. Germany)	✓		✓	✓	✓	✓	✓	✓	✓	
Unimens – Pharmanova/Unipharm (Switzerland)	✓		✓	✓	✓	✓	✓	✓	✓	
Yermonil – Ciba-Geigy (Switzerland)	e					✓	✓	✓	✓	

[a] Including functional sterility or endocrine infertility, dysfunctional uterine bleeding, premenopausal disturbances.
[b] Such as presence or history of venous inflammation, venous blood clots, hemorrhagic stroke, cerebrovascular disease, myocardial infarction (heart attack).
[c] Such as undiagnosed vaginal bleeding, jaundice, emotional disease; caution in asthma, epilepsy, migraine, heart or kidney function.
[d] "Oral anovulatory agent for family planning."
[e] "Anovulatory agent."

listed for Africa. Many of these products represent merely different dosage forms of the same ingredients.

There is one standard indication: contraception. (A special high-dosage form is also approved in some countries for the treatment of endometriosis, a painful disease which occurs when tissue that normally lines the uterus develops in other parts of the body.)

The same list of warnings is presented for all of these products, pointing particularly to the risk of thromboembolic changes in the blood vessels, the presence of proved or suspected cancers dependent on hormones for their growth, and liver disease or impaired liver function.

In Indonesia, Malaysia/Singapore, the Philippines, and Central America, labeling seems to follow different rules, or there are no rules at all. For the 10 products listed in Indonesia, for example, 6 carry recommendations for use only to prevent pregnancy, while 4 advocate other applications. Of the 22 listed in Malaysia/Singapore, 6 propose multiple uses. Of the 9 in the Philippines, 5 suggest various applications. In Central America, 6 of 23 products give additional indications. In Central America, it may be observed that a number of companies do not use the term "contraception" but refer instead to anovulatory agents for use in family planning.

The same lack of consistency is evident in the case of warnings to be brought to the attention of physicians. In the case of 3 products in Indonesia, 10 in Malaysia/Singapore, 1 in the Philippines, and 1 in Central America, the listings give no warnings at all, or advise "see company literature." (Offering the latter advice may soothe the corporate conscience—"We warned them!"—but it has little practical value, since most physicians apparently do not have the time, the patience, or the willingness to ask for and read additional informational material.)

Similar inconsistencies are involved within individual companies. Thus, Schering AG of West Germany, one of the world's largest producers of oral contraceptives, gives reasonably extended warnings for all of its products in the United States, Great Britain, Africa, Indonesia, the Philippines, and Central America, but for only some of them in Malaysia/Singapore. The same kind of situation holds for the American firm Wyeth. The Dutch company Organon gives no specific warnings for some of its products in Indonesia and Malaysia/Singapore, but does so for others. No specific warnings are presented by the Indonesian company Kalbe Farma in Indonesia. Syntex, headquartered in Panama, gives specific warnings for all of its contraceptives except for one in

Malaysia/Singapore. In the Third World, if there are any national regulatory agency rules or individual company policies to explain these
differences, they are not readily discernible.

"Throughout the world," we were told by one typical drug company
official, "our labeling is dictated in each country by the drug regulatory
agency of that country." In much of the Third World at least, as is seen
in table 8, this is just not true.

Only a few examples have been presented in this chapter to illustrate
the irrational, inconsistent, and sometimes potentially deadly promotion
and labeling of drug products and drug-dumping in developing countries. Many hundreds of others could be cited. In one way or another,
this kind of promotion can lead to irrational drug prescribing and drug
use, and to needless injury or death. These points seem evident:

*Many products ousted from the market in such industrialized nations
as the United States and Great Britain, or never approved for marketing, are readily available and widely promoted in the Third World.*
Among these are products containing clioquinol, aminopyrine, dipyrone,
and an assortment of combinations of vitamins, minerals, amino acids,
and such ingredients as ginseng, arsenic, strychnine, and royal bee jelly.
It should be borne in mind, however, that some products—notably those
needed for certain tropical infections—were never *disapproved* in the
industrialized nations. They were never proposed for approval.

*With many important products, the dangers of serious or lethal side
effects are minimized, glossed over, or totally ignored.* In the case of
some drugs that can produce serious injury or death, specific warnings
to physicians are included in the labeling in some Third World countries but not in others. Included here are such effects as the serious or
deadly blood damage produced by chloramphenicol, aminopyrine, and
dipyrone, the crippling and blindness associated with clioquinol, the
growth-stunting in children and the masculinization caused in girls and
women by anabolic hormones, and the serious or fatal blood clots caused
by oral contraceptives. Even in the case of the identical product marketed by the identical manufacturer, appropriate warnings may be given in
one Third World country but not in another.

*With many of these drugs, claims of effectiveness are wildly exaggerat-
ed.* For example, no adequate scientific evidence is available to support
the recommended use of anabolic hormones to increase strength or enhance athletic ability, or the application of so-called tonics to increase

physical and mental prowess, improve memory, enhance sexual ability, or promote a happy disposition. Perhaps more important, there is no adequate evidence to support the use of potentially damaging or deadly antibiotics for the treatment of trivial infections.

In the developing countries, the reliability of drug-labeling practices is not necessarily related to the size or type of company. Instances of irrational and potentially dangerous promotion have been apparent in the case of products marketed by some brand-name firms and by some generic-name companies, by some multinational companies and by some domestic companies, and by some based in capitalist countries and some in the communist bloc. The offending drug companies seem to demonstrate one characteristic in common, an acute deficiency of social responsibility.

It seems to be beyond dispute, as we have emphasized elsewhere,[81] that the use of drugs in the Third World has done far more good than harm. But harm has been done. Unfortunately, neither the good nor the harm can be described precisely. The extent of drug-induced injury and drug-induced death in developing countries has not been adequately investigated. If, however, the nature of adverse drug reactions in these countries is even roughly similar to the situation in the United States with its population of more than 200 million, where drugs have been implicated in several million cases of drug toxicity and at least 100,000 drug-related deaths each year,[82] then drugs may be responsible for a minimum of 10 to 15 million cases of injury and a million drug deaths annually among the more than 3 billion people in the Third World. But the situations are not strictly comparable. On the one hand, because of limited funds and inadequate drug supplies, per capita drug use is less in the developing countries. Hospitalization, often involving intensive drug therapy, is less common. On the other hand, some drugs considered to be unsafe for use in the United States are readily available, and widely used, in developing countries. Because of drug company marketing practices, together with the inability or unwillingness of Third World governments to enact and enforce adequate regulations, the labeling and promotion of many products in those nations often fail to disclose hazards and to include appropriate warnings. Hospital facilities for the treatment of life-threatening reactions are rarely accessible. If these facilities do exist, they can seldom be reached in time. The adverse-drug-reaction problem in the Third World warrants investigation.

3

THE PROFESSIONALS:
PHYSICIANS, PHARMACISTS,
AND OTHERS

"In my country, there are now not enough physicians, and there never were. Perhaps there never will be. But our big difficulty today is that most of the doctors we do have are in the wrong places."

— A public health official in Brazil

"Some days, I must see and try to diagnose and order a prescription for twenty or twenty-five patients in sixty minutes. Some days, it is worse."

— A clinic physician in Indonesia

"On my schedule, who has time to read a book, to look at a medical journal, to consult with a colleague who is expert? It is easier — and far quicker — to ask a drug company representative."

— A hospital-based physician in Nigeria

In the United States, there are about 300,000 physicians for a population of more than 200 million, or a ratio of roughly 1:600. The ratio in Great Britain is 1:750. It is generally the same in other industrialized nations. In Singapore, well on the way to development, it is 1:1,250. But it is 1:8,700 in Malaysia, 1:13,600 in Indonesia, 1:17,500 in Tanzania, and 1:34,000 in Mozambique. (See Table 1.) For some health professionals in some countries, the problem may be worse. In Tanzania, for example, there is reportedly one dentist for each 340,000,[1] and one dentist for each 500,000 in North Yemen.[2]

The shortages of physicians throughout the Third World have been made more grievous by problems of maldistribution. Most physicians are concentrated in the big cities, in or around the big teaching or referral hospitals and similar institutions. Most of them seem to prefer it that way. Laboratory and other facilities are reasonably available. Living is more comfortable, and remuneration may be better. But while most physicians are in the cities, most patients are elsewhere—and sometimes far elsewhere. In the rural areas, most of the ill never see a physician; they receive their care from more or less well trained nurses or physician assistants who work under the nominal supervision of a physician. These supervisors have little direct impact on the day-by-day activities of village clinics and dispensaries—they make only infrequent visits—but they can have enormous power in deciding which treatments shall be provided and, of key importance, which drug products shall be purchased by the government.

As we have noted earlier,[3] the physicians in Latin America appear to belong broadly in one of two groups. There are the first-class practitioners who keep up-to-date with the leading medical journals, foreign and domestic, who keep modern scientific monographs and textbooks in their offices, and who read them, who attend scientific meetings, and who consult regularly with their knowledgeable colleagues. Usually, they work in or close to a hospital or a medical school. They have access to a good library and use it. They rarely if ever seek or accept advice or guidance from a drug industry detailer or representative. They practice a quality of medicine that is about as high as the best available in New York or London or San Francisco.

On the other hand, there are those who received inadequate medical training, who have not opened a textbook since they passed their medical examinations, who do not read the journals, who avoid scientific meetings, who practically never consult with their colleagues, and whose main source of drug information is the company detailer. The kind of medicine they practice is generally as bad as the poorest that can be found in the United States and Britain. It seems clear that these two classes of physicians can be readily identified throughout the world.

Also evident in developing countries are some zealous physicians, most of them trained in Europe and America, who return to their native land and insist on bringing back with them the newest of the new in Western medicine. They call enthusiastically for open-heart-surgery facilities, diagnostic CT (Computerized Tomography) scanners, expensive kidney dialysis machines, facilities for organ transplantation, the latest radio-isotope equipment for diagnosis and therapy, and other high-technology devices.

Such costly installations have already been made—perhaps too many of them—in numerous medical centers in the United States and other industrialized areas, but this has usually been done without requiring significant slashes in the budget for less glamorous but more widely needed health services and equipment. In the developing countries, however, with their already limited resources, any investment in these technological marvels means dramatic benefits for a few fortunate individuals, but even less help for the hundreds of thousands or millions who suffer from tuberculosis, malaria, dysentery, malnutrition, and the other common plagues. Some developing countries have nonetheless been induced by one means or another to invest in high-cost, high-technology equipment. For instance, a kidney dialysis unit in Nepal was presumably built largely because of one high-ranking Nepalese politician who was afflicted with kidney disease. Such judgments are open to serious question. In many instances, it has proved impossible for native technicians to repair the equipment and keep it in operating condition, or to obtain replacement parts, and it lies, dust-covered, rusting, and idle, in a hospital storeroom. "Which, in the long run," comments one African health expert, "may be a blessing for our patients."

For most physicians in Africa, Asia, and Latin America, the problem is not a lack of modern super-gadgetry, but a shortage of the simpler yet essential facilities for diagnosis and treatment. Clinical laboratory facilities are often woefully inadequate, making it difficult to reach the appropriate diagnosis and determine which drug or other treatment is indicated. Such a deficiency may make it difficult or impossible to identify a serious or fatal adverse drug reaction.[4]

"It is exceedingly troublesome to show that a particular drug has caused a dangerously low white blood cell count, or a low red cell count," notes a pediatrician in Kenya, "if you can't do a blood cell count at all."[5]

A colleague in Tanzania adds, "This allows a lot of companies to defend their product by saying, 'Well, you know, nobody is reporting any evidence that our drug is really harmful.' We can point out that the evidence has already been printed in *Lancet,* or the *Biochemische Zeitschrift,* or the *New England Journal of Medicine,* but few doctors in these poor countries ever see such journals."[6]

Another deficiency is the shortage of time. Ayodele Tella of the University of Lagos says:

In Nigeria practically every physician—especially every physician in private practice—must see so many patients every day that he has little time to read journals, or study, or contemplate. It is hard for him to decline to see patients so that he can find some time to learn from scientists. It is so easy for him to get all his information—predigested—from a company representative. We pray that every company person will have all the facts and tell them honestly and fully. Unfortunately, our prayers have not always been answered.[7]

An American physician working for the Agency for International Development in Tanzania has reported physicians seeing one or two dozen patients per hour, and sometimes spending one minute per patient.[8] In other Third World countries, observers have been accustomed to watching a physician write the prescription—having already arrived at a diagnosis—while the patient is just beginning to describe his complaints.

The physicians in the developing countries are not only overworked, forced to see too many patients in too little time, ill-equipped with necessary laboratory support, and unable in most instances to keep up with medical science. They are also poorly paid. Accordingly, they have a strong incentive to maintain a virtual monopoly over not only the prescribing of drugs but also over the dispensing of drugs. The doctors, especially those in private practice, prescribe the drug—for a fee. They then sell the drug—for a fee.

This practice has irked pharmacists, who feel they have been relegated to the status of second-class professionals. It has restricted their activities to such duties as dispensing dentifrices, skin lotions, and aspirin and other over-the-counter medications. Many and probably most pharmacists, however, have consistently ignored the law by dispensing drugs without a prescription and even prescribing and occasionally injecting the drugs themselves.

Physicians usually defend their stand by such charges as "You cannot count on a pharmacist to fill the prescription correctly" or "I can't depend on the quality of the products they keep in stock." In some European countries, such as in parts of France and Belgium, similar vestigial attitudes still exist. "It is traditional," a Belgian village physician explained to us in 1981. "My father, who was a doctor, practiced it so. His father before him did the same." Some physicians in Europe and Japan, and in the Third World, put the explanation more simply: "We need the money." (In Japan, it was this attitude which was blamed in considerable part for the Japanese epidemic of SMON.)

The drug industry has been pleased to take advantage of such concepts, and has provided physicians with free samples in great abundance. Theoretically, such samples are intended to let doctors become familiar with a new product. In developing countries, however, both new and old products are offered at no cost, or at substantial discounts. There appears to be complete understanding that most physicians will sell these free or low-cost samples to their patients at full market price and then pocket the proceeds as an addition to their regular professional fee.

The free-sample device has become a major incentive to over-prescribing, to the use of overly high-priced products, to the ordering of drugs in unnecessarily large quantities, and to the use of a drug when no drug is clinically justifiable.[9] But the industry has learned that free-sampling can pay off handsomely. It costs the companies relatively little. Most important, it wins the friendship and support of the medical profession.

Rational prescribing is defined as ordering the right drug for the right patient, at the right time and in the right amounts, with due consideration of costs. Clinical pharmacologists and other drug experts in the Third World are among the first to label much of the prescribing in their countries as irrational.[10] The examples are numerous and disquieting:

— prescribing multiple hormones, multiple antibiotics, and similar combinations when only a single drug is clinically indicated;

— prescribing any antibiotic in the treatment of "flu" or the common cold;

— prescribing a newly-introduced drug solely on the grounds that it is new;

— declining to prescribe or dispense a high-quality, low-cost generic-name product in place of a costly brand-name product—which may or may not be of high quality—on the grounds that "the generic firms can't be trusted" (such prescribers and pharmacists are apparently unaware that the generic and the brand-name versions may be made by the same firm);

— giving a drug by injection rather than by mouth because "our people prefer it that way—we belong to an 'injection culture.'" (Patients and physicians alike have been duped by rumors and hush-hush campaigns suggesting that aspirin is too dangerous for most children—"You doctors in Europe and America do not seem to know this"—and should be replaced with a costly and more hazardous substitute, preferably given by injection.)

One characteristic of most Third World drug use is the stubborn resistance of physicians and pharmacists against telling the patient what drug is being given. Including the identity of the product in the label is simply not done. In general, the patient is told only how many times a day to take the medicine, and perhaps whether to take it before or after meals. In a few cases, the label may give the name of the drug, but only in Latin, or it may carry such a cryptic description as "mixture" or "elixir." Physicians and pharmacists alike have defended this practice:

> "If the patient needed a refill, he might try to buy it for less money on the black market."
> "We have some very inquisitive patients who might go in the library and check for the side effects."
> "If the patient knew the identity of the drug he was taking, it might not work."[11]

In some countries, like Singapore, the situation is now changing, and physicians are becoming more willing to identify the drug in the label.[12] In Kenya, Karuga Koinange, Director of Medical Services, has recently called for full labeling of all prescription drugs, including the identification of the active ingredients, complete instructions for proper use, appropriate storage conditions, and the expiration date, after which the medicine should be discarded. His proposals received heated denunciation from both physicians and pharmacists. Koinange told us, "Well, you have to start somewhere. Everyone is entitled to know what medicines he takes."[13]

In most of the developing countries, any attempt to minimize irrational prescribing, curb the needless multiplicity of products on the market, and reduce expenditures is strongly attacked by medical leaders—and simultaneously by drug company spokesmen. It is assailed as an intolerable interference with the doctor's God-given right to make clinical judgments without any objection from anyone, and to prescribe as he and he alone sees fit.

Together, industry and medical leaders have insisted particularly that nothing be done to reduce the number of drug products, now counted in the thousands, that are on the market. This deluge of drugs would appear to offer no clinical advantages but rather represent a pollution of the pharmaceutical environment. Many medical leaders have steadfastly refused to face up to the fact that the more products on the market, the more difficult it is for an individual physician to learn about their values and their dangers. John Yudkin claims:

> The justification which is often given for the existence of all these drugs and drug forms is that they permit the doctor "freedom to choose" the most appropriate drug for each patient. Yet we have already seen how the freedom to choose may often mean that the doctor can prescribe a costly brand-name product when a less expensive form of equivalent quality is available under its generic name. It may mean that he will order a costly product instead of a different drug at a lower cost which will give essentially the same clinical results. The only difference that often exists between a range of similar drugs is the quality or quantity of their advertising. Moreover, such "freedom" permits a physician to order a fixed combination of drugs when only one can be clinically justified, or when individual dose adjustment is necessary.[14]

Industry-backed medical opposition to improving prescribing habits became familiar to Americans during a series of extended Senate hearings in the late 1950s and 1960s which, among other things, looked into the prescribing habits of physicians. These habits came under scathing attack from some of the most respected pharmacologists and other drug experts in the country. The don't-tell-me-how-to-prescribe attitude of the American Medical Association, backed by the U.S. Pharmaceutical Manufacturers Association, received a traumatic drubbing in the Senate—and later in the nation's press.[15] Such a confrontation is yet to come in the Third World. When it does come, it may be predicted with some degree of confidence that it will be hemorrhagic.

Pharmacists in the Third World, and also in parts of Europe, have not yet won the status they have achieved in the United States and the United Kingdom. This is doubly unfortunate. Modern pharmacists have studied hard to learn modern pharmacy, and they deserve recognition. Even sadder, they can contribute far more to effective health care than they are now allowed to do.

In the United States, it is increasingly evident that pharmacists are

generally the drug experts on the health team. Many are more knowledgeable about drugs than are most physicians, and American and British physicians are increasingly leaning on pharmacists for advice and
guidance on product selection and drug use. Restricting their duties to
"count, fill, pour, and type," or to ordinary merchandising—selling everything from cosmetics and liquor to camera equipment and garden
tools—is now seen as a waste of skilled manpower in the field of health
which cannot be afforded even by rich nations. Wasting their abilities in
poor countries is particularly unpardonable.

In many developing countries, pharmacy is restricted primarily to the
large cities, and there are few pharmacies in towns and villages. In the
cities, there is open warfare: physicians declare that pharmacists cannot
be trusted, and pharmacists respond by claiming that physicians are
stuffing their own pockets by selling drugs themselves and also charging
too much.

Perhaps understandably, pharmacists have retaliated by assuming—
illegally—some physician functions. They diagnose, they prescribe, they
dispense. It is, of course, against the law for a pharmacist to dispense a
prescription drug—an antibiotic, a drug for high blood pressure, a hormone, a contraceptive pill, a drug for duodenal ulcer—without a physician's prescription.

"That is a crazy law," says a Mexico City pharmacist. "If a customer
needs some hormone for his asthma, I will sell it to him without a
prescription. Even if he is a policeman."

A Nigerian health official told us, "Here, one can obtain any drug—
any prescription drug—without a prescription. Naturally, this is against
the law. But you can get it—*anything!*"

"Even a narcotic?"

"If you know the shop, just wait until the boss looks the other way.
Anything!"

In small communities that have no pharmacy, both over-the-counter
and prescription drugs—obtainable, of course, without prescription—
can usually be purchased at a general store, usually from an untrained
clerk. A reporter for the *Wall Street Journal* described the procedure in
one such establishment:

> Does the clerk have penicillin? He turns to root through a drawer behind
> his counter and, finding no pills, only penicillin ointment, offers a conso-
> lation: a bottle of colorless liquid that, according to its label, contains

dissolved rhinoceros horn. It promises immediate relief from malaria, higher temperature fever affecting heart and four limbs, climate giddiness, insanity, toothache, etc.[16]

Various risks lie in wait for the customer who patronizes one of the "street dealers" or "street pharmacists" who offer their pharmaceutical services on the streets before bus stations, markets, and general stores. There is no way to determine the identity, strength, purity, or even cleanliness of the pills or potions they display in opened, unlabeled packets or bottles.

"You can't tell if it is the antimalarial you requested or merely aspirin or an antacid," claims a Zambian health worker. "Has the shelf life expired? How should the drug be used? Is it safe for children? The salesman gives you whatever answer he thinks will make you happy."[17]

The matter of shelf life can be extremely important especially in the tropics where many important drugs can quickly become useless or even toxic in the heat. Some products which can be kept on a pharmacy shelf for several years in temperate climates will lose their potency in a few months in the tropics.[18] An ethical pharmacist will take any product with an expired shelf-life and return it for credit to his supplier, who will presumably destroy it. A less ethical pharmacist—or supplier—may sell it at a discount to a street salesman.

Even a drug product with a seemingly informative label can present problems. Thus, in Malaysia, the Consumers Association of Penang has found Johnson & Johnson baby-powder containers filled locally with perfumed flour.[19]

In virtually every developing country, an especially strategic role is played by the traditional healers—the herb doctors of Asia, Africa, and Latin America. In nations where orthodox or Western physicians are few and overworked, and usually concentrated in big-city hospitals, the traditional healers are comparatively easy to find in the villages. They are available—and they are trusted. Many of them have spent long years of apprenticeship to acquire their knowledge and their skills. Some of their herb or animal-extract remedies have been widely and successfully applied for centuries or even thousands of years.

Ayodele Tella of the University of Lagos in Nigeria has this to say:

> In the rural areas, the people live very close to traditional medicine. If the traditional healer is at your doorstep, and the doctor you might want to see lives far away, you use the traditional healer. One wants to encour-

age that sort of thing, but with necessary safeguards. I personally would
like to see these healers given at least some training in an educational
system.[20]

In Nigeria and other countries, government leaders are trying to stimulate the use of traditional medicine. It seems that traditional healers
can learn from Western medicine much that would be helpful. At the
same time, modern drug experts believe, there is much that Western
physicians can learn from traditional healers. Any efforts to control traditional medicine must be handled with great delicacy, for this is a highly sensitive area and the traditionalists have considerable political
power.

Yet, to the dismay of leaders of traditional medicine, some dealers in
herbs and other old, established remedies are apparently yielding to the
temptation of making a fast rupee or peso. In Malaysia, the Consumers
Association of Penang tested products labeled "elixir of rhinoceros
horn" and found no trace of rhinoceros horn or any other part of the
animal.[21] Other traditional products have been spiked with antibiotics,
steroid hormones, aminopyrine, and dipyrone.[22] In Sri Lanka, the label
of one product states: "For fever . . . use crushed leaves, and the fever
comes down in three days." What the label does not disclose is that the
remedy also includes aspirin.[23] In Singapore, a study revealed that nearly thirty commonly used Chinese herbal remedies contained toxic quantities of arsenic.[24]

Throughout the Third World, each practicing physician is responsible—either directly or through the assistants he supervises—for the care
of many more patients than is the case in countries like the United
States and Great Britain. This means that each physician in a developing country has an inordinately strategic role in determining which
drugs shall be ordered and prescribed. In such a situation, the Third
World physician becomes an exceedingly attractive target for promotion
by the drug industry—and, if the occasion should arise, for bribery.

4

THE DRUG INDUSTRY

If a man should make a better mousetrap, Ralph Waldo Emerson said long ago, the world will beat a path to his door. But if the new mousetrap is not better than the old, what then? Facing this kind of dilemma, the drug industry has found a remarkably satisfactory answer: double the advertising budget.

Over the past few decades, the drug industry has produced hundreds of new drugs and drug products that are now being marketed widely in both developed and developing nations. The overwhelming proportion of these, it may be noted, have been the creations of research-oriented multinational firms. They have not come from domestic companies—large as some of these may be—or from those multinational companies that have contributed little to new drug development but much to the marketing of low-cost and generally high-quality competitive versions.

Among these new discoveries are drugs that can effectively and sometimes dramatically control many of the major diseases that have long plagued the Third World: malaria, typhoid fever, typhus, cholera, bubonic plague, tuberculosis, trachoma, gonorrhea and syphilis. Less remarkable advances have been made against such tropical ills as filariasis, schistosomiasis (or bilharziasis), African sleeping sickness (or trypanosomiasis), and ascaris infestation.

Industry leaders have lamented that they have been given little credit for their accomplishments. Instead, especially in the Third World, they have been constantly berated for their pricing and other marketing practices, their supposedly extortionate profits, and for generally exploiting the poorer nations of the world. They have been denounced for their failure to invest more effort in tropical-disease research.

Part of this industry complaint may be justified. The drug companies have not received enormous praise—except self-praise—for their good deeds. On the other hand, company spokesmen have invited much of this criticism. They have not shown any great eagerness to share much if any credit with university, government, and other nonindustry researchers who discovered some of the new drugs themselves, or who provided the basic knowledge underlying many of the industry's breakthrough discoveries.

The pricing structure used by the multinational drug corporations in developing countries has been the subject of much criticism and confusion.[1] Observers have been puzzled to learn that American firms sometimes charge less for their products in the Third World than they do in the United States, sometimes charge more, and sometimes charge more for some products but less for others. Whether or not such practices are justifiable may be debated. There appears to be no agreement on whether a company is morally or economically obligated to charge less to customers who are poor—especially those who are poor and sick. Is there a comparable obligation on companies like General Electric, Exxon, Sony, General Foods, Toyota, British Petroleum, Fiat, and Volkswagen?

How should an American, a European, or a Japanese corporation set its pricing structure in a country in which foreign investments may be seized at any time, plants may be expropriated, prices may be drastically controlled, and international patents are already ignored?

What should be done about arrangements under which a subsidiary in a Latin American country, for example, buys a drug supply from its parent at an enormous markup and then sells it in Guatemala or Brazil at a slightly higher price (still beyond the reach of many patients) in order to show only a small profit for tax purposes?[2]

These and other problems are of great concern to ethicists, economists, political scientists, consumer groups, government leaders, and industry critics and defenders alike. In addition, there are two controversial issues which are of special interest to drug experts:

— How much should be invested by the multinational companies in the development of drugs or vaccines to battle tropical diseases, especially if those products would have no substantial sales in industrialized nations?

— What, if anything, should be done to limit or control the marketing, and particularly the heavy promotion in developing countries, of drug products which have only minimal clinical value, or none at all, *in those countries?*

The amount of money currently being spent by the major multinationals on tropical-disease research is itself a matter of debate. Estimates range from as low as $30 million to perhaps $40 million, $50 million, or more a year. Even the smallest of the figures might appear to be substantial, yet, when measured against a total research investment by the world's drug industry of several billions, the expenditure of a few tens of millions annually to benefit nearly three-fourths of the world's population would scarcely seem to be exorbitant.

There may be a cynical, callous, but economically sound explanation for this lack of support for tropical-disease research: it could not pay for itself for a very long time. The research director of a drug company based in the United States declares:

> Of course, we could go into a big program on, say, tropical sleeping sickness or Chagas' disease. We might put in three, or four, or five million dollars a year. In five or ten years, we might hit on a useful new compound that could help a lot of people in Africa or South America. They would like to have it, but neither they nor their government could afford to pay much for it. They have the disease but not the money. My stockholders would have my scalp.

It is conceivable that the people in the Third World are poor because they are ill and cannot do productive work. If they were healthy, perhaps they could produce more and be able to pay their bills, and thus everyone would benefit. But this line of reasoning does not seem to appeal to most corporate managers and their shareholders.

It is also conceivable that drug companies in socialist or communist-bloc countries, being supposedly less greedy for profits, might be more willing to invest in such philanthropic activities. No willingness of this kind, however, has yet been notably apparent.

Certainly, at least in the United States, great interest has been expressed in drug-industry profit rates, for many years among the highest for all manufacturing industries.[3] Whether consideration is given to net profits (after taxes) as based on sales or on investment, the profit record of American companies has been remarkably bright. In good times and bad, in depressions, recessions, and boom years, virtually every major drug company has remained profitable. Profits in some developing countries may be even higher. In Indonesia, Iwan Darmansjah declares, "Reports on the big drug companies abroad state that they make 9 percent net profits after taxation, but in Indonesia it seems that 10 to 20 percent net profits are usual."[4] Stung by criticism of their higher profits and prices, industry spokesmen have consistently defended their practices by insisting that their profits *had* to be high in order to make possible their research. Conveniently, they usually ignored the fact—obvious to any accountant—that net profits are those remaining *after* all research costs have been paid.

It is our view that "profits" is not necessarily a dirty word. Prices must be high enough to finance the research essential for improved health care and improved health in the future. These opinions are apparently acceptable in industrialized countries, where most people seem aware of the need for more effective agents, especially to control such diseases of "advanced civilization" as high blood pressure, coronary disease, and cancer. But such views are less popular in the Third World.

A Zambian drug official told one company representative:

> You say you must charge such steep prices in my country so you can do research. We want you to do those investigations—but on the diseases that afflict *our* people. But your scientists work on things like heart disease and carcinoma. These are now of little importance in Zambia. What you want us to do is pay tribute to help sick people in Switzerland and England and the United States. This is not fair.

Another industry attitude which has received a chilly reception in several African countries is expressed this way: "You people would have enough money to pay for all the medicines you need if you wouldn't waste so much buying military aircraft and automatic rifles, or subsidizing your national airline." Such criticisms overlook the fact that, justifiable or not, few African or Asian nations display much trust in their neighbors, and most live in fear of invasion or revolution. In the same way, a national airline may not be justifiable on economic grounds, but countries in the Third World—like those in advanced parts of the world—have a need for a boost to national morale.

At least as complex is the problem of wasting grievously limited health care funds, private or governmental, to purchase drugs that are needlessly unsafe, relatively ineffective, needlessly expensive, or simply needless. These are the products that represent a less-than-better mousetrap.

Many of these are what have been termed "me-too" drugs, usually created by making a trivial change in the molecule of the parent drug, yielding a new drug that is no safer, no more effective, and no less costly—and is sometimes more costly—than the parent compound, but is changed sufficiently to win a patent. (Me-too products do not include generic-name versions of the original substance. Generics are discussed later in this chapter.)

Many are fixed-ratio combination products which, with only a few exceptions, present trivial if any clinical advantages and may involve additional dangers to health and life. In most instances, drug experts agree, these combination products are primarily a marketing gimmick: they permit an ingenious manufacturer to take two or more drugs no longer protected by patent, combine them, and promote them under a catchy new name, which can be monopolized indefinitely. Darmansjah says:

> Over 50 percent of drugs on the market constitute fixed combinations. Very few have documented and established evidence to show their superiority over their single active ingredients. Drug companies are promoting them through a fierce competition which sometimes neglects the ethical aspects of medicine.

There are also products which may have unquestioned value in industrialized countries but which have only limited worth in the Third World. One example includes drugs required especially for the elderly. Another includes expensive vitamin combinations and other nutritive supplements being touted for use by poor populations, whose major nutritive need is not for vitamins but for food.

"It is indecent the way that the companies make their salesmen push vitamins in my country," claims a Tanzanian mother, Fatumo Mrisho, in Dar es Salaam. "They have tricked doctors into prescribing them not only for malnutrition but for everything else."

One day, Mrs. Mrisho told us, she took her young daughter to a physician in another city to find out why the child was suffering from violent nausea and vomiting.

"The girl must be given vitamins," the doctor said. "I will write you a prescription."

"That is nonsense," she said. "My daughter has not been malnourished. She is suffering from vomiting. She does not need vitamins."

"Who are you to say she does not need vitamins?"

"I say so. My specialty is nutrition. Also, I am a physician myself."

Later, she related to us, "He was most awfully offended. He would have nothing further to do with us. But I cannot blame him too much. He had believed the company advertising."

In Indonesia, there is a similar criticism of the intense promotion of vitamins. "Our people have a desperate need for proteins, for calories, not for vitamins," says Darmansjah. "But Hoffmann-La Roche in Switzerland, Squibb in the United States, and the other big vitamin companies apparently have a greater need for sales and profits." To some observers, the underlying problem is that the major companies, both multinational and domestic, have not tried to suit their products to meet the drug needs of the developing countries. Instead, the firms have aimed at finding markets for their high-cost brand-name products, gearing their promotion to the creation of a demand for them.[5] In such promotional campaigns, many supposedly prestigious companies have descended to the use of puffed-up claims, the minimizing of hazards, and the dissemination of testimonials, often slanted or actually fictitious, which are bought from physicians and patients.

Several years ago, we reported that the cost of drug promotion in the United States was larger than the cost of medical education.[6] Drug promotion in Africa, Asia, and Latin America appears to be even more intense.

Some of these maneuvers have been analyzed in earlier chapters. Labeling practices of multinational companies marketing a number of important antiarthritis agents, antipsychotic tranquilizers, drugs to control depression, and antiepilepsy products in Latin America have previously been described.[7] These are, however, not the only examples that could be presented. There are many others:

— In Africa, clonidine was marketed as Catapres by Boehringer Ingelheim as a useful and sometimes dramatically effective agent to control high blood pressure. In the United States and Great Britain, physicians were warned that treatment must be terminated gradually. If a dose were omitted for twelve hours or more after it was supposed to be given, the result could be a sudden overshoot of blood pressure and possibly brain hemorrhage. Not until this omission was described by John Yudkin did the firm disclose the appropriate warning to Third World physicians.[8]

— Bayer's ampicillin was described in a 1980 advertisement in *Modern Medicine of Asia* as "the key to success in modern antibiotic therapy ... can be used without risk of toxicity." A scientific report by a team of investigators in Bangladesh, however, disclosed that more than 7 percent of patients treated with ampicillin showed toxic side effects. Ironically, both the advertisement and the scientific report were published in the same issue of the same journal.[9]

— In North Yemen, a syrup containing calcium, vitamin D, and vitamin B12 has been marketed by the British firm Glaxo as Calci-Ostelin B12. The calcium and the vitamin D are indicated for rickets, which is a problem in the country largely because Yemeni children are kept heavily clothed to protect them from the sun. Rickets, however, can be readily prevented at much lower cost by the use of inexpensive calcium and vitamin D preparations. The inclusion of vitamin B12 is puzzling. Its only recognized use is in the prevention or treatment of pernicious anemia, which is reportedly rare in Yemen. One Yemeni physician declared he had never seen a case. Nevertheless, the Glaxo promotion includes statements like these: "The tonic value of vitamin B12 has steadily become established in recent years. . . . Vitamin B12 can stimulate growth processes, promoting physical vigour, alertness and general well-being, particularly in young children whose development has been held back by any deficiency of this vitamin in the diet or by inability to absorb it." A Glaxo official explained to an inquiring British physician that the claims were made only "in certain overseas countries where concepts of medicine and therapeutics held by doctors, pharmacists and the public are very different from ours."[10] The role played by Glaxo and other drug companies in creating those "very different" concepts has not been examined. One cynical pharmacologist put the matter this way: "Well, a mother spending her last few pennies to buy B12 for her hungry baby can be assured that the child won't get pernicious anemia while it dies from starvation."

— In Kenya, physicians have expressed their concern over radio adver-

tising to promote the use of Vaseline products, some of them perfumed, as skin creams for babies. Dermatologists and pediatricians
are alarmed by the occurrence of what they call "Vaseline derma-
titis." One doctor claims, "In the advertising, they make the listen-
er feel that application of the ointment can be equated with mother love."

— Pentazocine, marketed by Winthrop/Sterling under the name of
Talwin, has been advertised with such phrases as "controls pain
without addiction" and "generally well-tolerated even by elderly
and very ill patients." But, as pharmacologists Matthew Gwee
and T. S. Yeoh of the University of Singapore have stated, various
authorities have reported that the drug can cause serious problems
of drug addiction. In equally effective doses, pentazocine causes at
least as many adverse effects as does morphine.[11]

It has long been abundantly clear that one of the simplest and most
effective ways to cut drug costs and drug expenditures would be the use
of a low-cost generic-name product in place of a high-cost brand-name
version. This could be accomplished by urging physicians to prescribe
by generic name in the first place, or by authorizing and inducing pharmacists to select a generic product as a substitute for the brand-name
product actually prescribed.

Such product selection would permit the substitution of a generic
competitor for the brand-name product containing the identical active
ingredient. It would, for example, allow a pharmacist to replace Winthrop's brand-name phenobarbital, marketed as Luminal, with another
phenobarbital made by a different manufacturer. It would *not* permit
the replacement of phenobarbital with pentobarbital or chloral hydrate
or aspirin.

Noting that some generic products were being sold at prices 60, 70, or
even 80 percent below the price of their respective brand-name counter-
parts, some enthusiasts have proclaimed that generic substitution could
save 60, 70 or 80 percent of total drug expenditures in the United
States. Such forecasts were quickly dampened.[12] In this country, at least
up to the late 1960s, most prescription drugs were still protected by
patent, and no generic forms could be legally marketed. Although the
percentage of savings on some products seemed relatively enormous,
there were other instances in which the savings would be more nearly

10 to 20 percent. Further, some American physicians were already accustomed to prescribe generically, and no savings could be achieved by requiring them to continue to do so.

Nevertheless, the possibility of making even small savings by the use of generics seemed alarming to most major brand-name companies. The latter could hardly dispute the price differences that existed. Instead, they turned their full attack on the quality of generics. Generic products, they charged, could not be depended on to provide the proper strength, the proper consistency, and the proper rate of absorption in patients; they represented, it was claimed, "second-class medicine."

The brutal fight over generics, with the brand-name firms and leaders of the American Medical Association pitted against generic houses and consumer advocates, along with their various allies and opponents in the Congress, was thus fought out over the issue of the quality of generic products. It was clear that, at least at some times in the past, some generic companies had made grievous errors in their manufacturing processes. It was also found that some of the brand-name firms had occasionally turned out defective batches, but this was not heavily stressed by the brand-name advocates.[13]

Then, in the late 1960s, the situation changed. Many of the major brand-name companies began to go into the generic business themselves. There was no philanthropic motive behind the move. One big company after another realized that the patents on its best money-making drugs were about to expire, and that competitors could legally market them soon as generics. Few big money-making new drugs were in the pipeline, about ready for market. Furthermore, each company recognized that its competitors were in approximately the same predicament, and that their products could be taken over and marketed. In the United States, at least, the "great generic controversy" had essentially ended. The brand-name firms could no longer dismiss generics as second-class products, since they were now selling generics.[14]

In Great Britain, the use of generics is gradually increasing, especially in hospitals. In most of Europe, however, significant acceptance of generics has not yet occurred.[15] But in the Third World countries, desperate as all of them are to reduce their relatively heavy drug expenditures, generic products remain essentially unaccepted.

The potential savings in cost are beyond question. In Sri Lanka, for example, Hoffmann-La Roche's Valium is priced at 90 cents per tablet, while the same drug marketed by an Indian firm as diazepam costs 2 cents per tablet. In 1974, the drug propanolol used for high blood pressure and heart arrhythmias could be obtained from a Polish supplier, and also from Imperial Chemicals as Inderal but at a price 456 times higher.[16] The Australian firm Nicholas has been selling its brand of aspirin known as Aspro at a price roughly six times that of generic aspirin. "With the very limited budgets in the Third World," it has been asserted, "it would be criminally insane to pressure them to buy Aspro rather than aspirin."[17]

As in the United States, the fight over generic substitution in the Third World is being waged mainly over the issue of product quality. So far, the brand-name firms have apparently convinced medical leaders by one means or another that the quality of generics cannot be trusted—that the generic products are second-class. It is undoubtedly true that some generics have been of low quality, and representatives of brand-name firms are quick to regale physicians with various horror stories, some of them true. It is also undoubtedly true that such honored brand-name companies as Pfizer in the United States, Burroughs-Wellcome in Great Britain, and Hoffmann-La Roche in Switzerland have been charged with marketing defective batches of their products, but this has usually not been mentioned.[18]

Some of these denunciations and counterdenunciations have had curious aspects. Thus, when the government in Kenya had been buying a tranquilizer from a firm in Israel, répresentatives of Hoffmann-La Roche warned that the bulk material used by the Israeli firm could not be trusted. "But," says Karuga Koinange of the Kenyan Ministry of Health, "the people in Israel had bought their material from Hoffmann-La Roche."[19]

In numerous cases, efforts of generic firms to sell their products in the Third World have been blocked by simple hard-currency problems. A Zambian official explains:

> Except where patent rights dictate otherwise, our purchases of drugs are conducted under the generic names by means of open tender. Profit margins are small due to the competitive nature of the tender system. Suppliers therefore demand payment by Letter of Credit. . . . Makers of branded products, however, cannot generally compete in price with the generic manufacturers but are usually prepared to supply their local agents on credit terms of 12–18 months, having added a compensatory element into their prices. Thus it has happened that when stocks of the generic drugs are not available, we have had no other option but to buy the branded product at comparatively high prices.[20]

This situation, along with the promotional practices of the foreign multinational companies, proved to be highly exasperating to some Indian officials.

"So why don't you throw them out of the country?" one of our colleagues asked an Indian drug official.

"Good God!" replied the official. "They would only be replaced by Indian companies, and that could be worse."[21]

It is believed by many, including many physicians, that advertising in medical journals and direct mailings to physicians represent the major forms of promotion used by the drug industry. These are, in fact, of relatively minor importance. The big drug firms have learned to put most of their promotion dollars into drug detailing, or frequent visits to physicians in their offices—and often in their homes.

The individuals who do this work are known variously as detail men in the United States, *visitadores* in Latin America, company representatives or "reps" in Europe and most of the countries in Africa and Asia, and "propas" (the Japanese term for propagandists) in parts of Southeast Asia. The ratio is roughly one detail man for ten or more physicians in the United States, Great Britain, and most of the Northern European countries, one to eight in Ecuador, one to five in Colombia, about one to four in Tanzania, and one to three in Guatemala, Mexico, and Brazil. Drug company officials in Indonesia and the Philippines put the ratio at one detail man for every two or three physicians.[22] Some detailers, since they are employed by private industry, are able to make more money than do the physicians on whom they call, especially young physicians who work in government health programs.

Some of the detail men in Third World nations have received only a secondary education, but they frequently pass themselves off as medical experts.[23] Others have received training in pharmacy or medicine. Says Ayodele Tella in Nigeria:

> Some of them were my students. It is outrageous that they were educated at public expense and then were hired by a drug company before they could repay society for training them. I tried to teach them that the drugs should be known by their generic names, so you can recognize the active agent. I tried to teach them that if the patient suffers a side effect and you did not give adequate advance information to the physicians or the pharmacist, then the blame is on you. But once our students leave us, sometimes within a year, they have forgotten the generic names, and also they forget to give the warnings.[24]

In Kenya, A. O. Obel of the University of Nairobi wrote, "Doctors must be warned of the persuasive language of pharmaceutical firm representatives who employ elaborate but doubtful if not baseless data to discredit established drugs in order to promote their own poorly evaluated agents."[25]

The drug companies proclaim that their representatives are supposed to inform physicians of the "proper and safe use of our products." Drug experts in medical schools and government agencies usually ridicule any such idea. "The *visitadores* are sort of 'traveling professors of therapeutics,'" said Silvestre Frenk in Mexico City. "They merely give a smooth, technical-sounding sales argument which they have memorized."[26]

It is commonly believed that the most valuable asset for any company representative is his relationship—as son, nephew, or son-in-law—to some influential medical leader or an important official in the health ministry.

In most developing countries, the detail men are often considered to be only salesmen. They have been repeatedly charged with exaggerating the claims and glossing over the dangers of their products, bulwarking their arguments by passing out copies of articles reprinted from journals that are actually owned or controlled by the drug company, and using rumors, innuendos, or outright lies to run down competitive products. They have induced physicians or purchasing agents, occasionally by offering bribes, kickbacks, or other inducements, to purchase drugs in enormous quantities, with the result that some of these drugs will spoil on the storage shelves long before they can be dispensed. In Tanzania, after such practices had been uncovered, the longtime Minister of Health, Leader Stirling, threatened to expel all company representatives from the country. "The people of Tanzania paid for their education," he told us just before he left office in 1980. "They showed their gratitude by selling out to the drug companies."[27]

A panel of drug company spokesmen expressed their horror at any such allegations of wrongdoing. They said:

> Medical reps disseminate scientific information on the use, advantages, and disadvantages of the drugs which they promote. We do not dictate to the authorities as to what should be ordered. . . . The suggestion that our visits to our trained and highly qualified doctors can result in proliferation of useless drugs would amount to questioning the integrity and intelligence of these doctors.[28]

If the integrity, intelligence, and knowledge of some of these physicians were questioned, many experts feel, it would be about time.

In Colombia, José Félix Patiño, one of the most highly regarded authorities on medical education in Latin America, former Minister of Health, and for many years executive director of the Panamerican Federation of Associations of Medical Schools, gave his view in these words:

> The situation here is very bad. Communication with our medical people is inadequate. We cannot reach them. It is the company representative, the *visitador,* who tells them how to prescribe. It is shocking to realize that the salesman has, in fact, become the prescriber. Medical education institutions and professional organizations, of course, have the primary responsibility to conducting continuing education for practicing physicians. They have only partly fulfilled this obligation.[29]

It is likewise shocking to hear some of the prescribing advice given by detail men to Third World physicians. One illustration—sadly, far from unique—was cited by an English nurse working in Bangladesh:

> My husband [a British physician] went into a doctor's office one day, just to have a chat with him, and there was a drug rep present, so Michael sat down and listened. . . . The drug rep was trying to persuade this rather young doctor that frusemide,* a drug that gets rid of excess fluid in the body, was a very good drug to use for children who had *kwashiorkor.* . . . This is a serious [protein] deficiency disease which produces swelling all over the body, and he was suggesting that this drug was very good at reducing this oedema. . . . My poor husband felt that he had to jump in at that point and say, "Well, alright, the swelling will go down because you, in fact, urinate frequently and you get rid of the fluid, but it will kill the child." And the drug representative said, "Well, the child is going to die anyway."[30]

For a decade or so, growing attention has been directed toward what has been loosely described as "drug-dumping." Presumably, it refers to the action of a company in selling to a developing country a drug that is not allowed on the market in the "country of origin." Unfortunately, the meaning of "country of origin" is no longer clear, and the term "drug-dumping" has become so confused that perhaps *it* should be dumped.

Whether the practice is rare or frequent, we believe that the phrase drug-dumping should be restricted to one meaning: *the marketing in*

---

*Known as frusemide in British publications, but as furosemide in the United States.

any country, Third World or not, of any drug once approved in an industrialized nation and later removed from the market because it was found to be ineffective, unsafe, or both. It should not be applied to products that were never submitted for approval to the Food and Drug Administration or similar agency. Such products must be considered to be *not approved,* but neither are they *disapproved.* Among them are many agents for the treatment of tropical infections; these could not be tested adequately in the United States to meet FDA requirements, primarily because the diseases are virtually nonexistent in the United States.

A number of drug products now being marketed and promoted in Third World countries clearly belong in the dumping category. They were removed from the U.S. market either by FDA action or by "voluntary action" by the company, under more or less pressure from FDA. Among these are various fixed-ratio antibiotic combinations; antipyretics and analgesics like aminopyrine and dipyrone; clioquinol; cough and cold remedies and linaments containing chloroform; and antihistamines containing methapyrilene.

The continued sale of such agents has been described on the one hand as an example of free enterprise at its best, and on the other as a disgraceful illustration of exploitation. Multinational companies based in the United States have come in for a large share of the blame for these practices. Consumer activists have insisted vehemently that the government should take steps to prevent drug-dumping by any American firm. But such a step, though it may appear to be desirable, cannot be taken easily. Although the Congress has authorized FDA to stop a company from exporting an unapproved or disapproved product, the company can easily set up a manufacturing or formulating plant overseas and ship its product from there. There seems to be considerable doubt that, under the Constitution, the Congress can halt such activities. It is important to note that, so far as we can determine, no industrialized country—not Great Britain, not Switzerland, not West Germany, not Japan, not the Netherlands, not Italy—and no communist-bloc country—has yet found a way to block drug-dumping.

According to those who speak for industry, the responsibility for protecting its own people must be taken by each Third World nation itself. Michael Peretz of the International Federation of Pharmaceutical Manufacturers Associations has declared that the responsibility for controlling drug company activity lies fairly and squarely with the Third

World governments.[31] A company official in Indonesia explained to us, "All we do is make a presentation on our product. It is up to the government to make the decision, freely and openly, to meet its own needs."

We questioned him about the "freely and openly." "You mean that you never lean a little bit—perhaps apply a bit of pressure here and there, or offer some inducement—to get a favorable decision?"

"Perhaps, a little bit," he said. "But that is a normal business practice."

Company representatives in Tanzania have denied that drug-dumping was reprehensible in any way. "There are *no* unsafe drugs in Tanzania," one of them told a reporter.[32]

In Tanzania and other developing nations, drug experts are horrified at the evil effects of drug-dumping, the squandering of scarce health-care funds, and especially the needless injuries and deaths caused by unsafe products. Most of these experts say they are virtually powerless to stop dumping.

"We have been able to stop a few bad drugs from getting on the market," says a pharmacologist at the University of the Philippines, "but it is exceptionally difficult to get rid of the drugs which are already allowed here. The companies are too firmly entrenched."

In Nigeria, says Ayodele Tella,

> we have a proposed new drug reviewed by a committee of experts—many of them highly competent people trained in England, Canada, the United States. They review all the evidence, both that submitted by the company and that published in the best scientific journals. They may decide that the proposed drug is not safe or not effective enough, and they reject the application. But then the company goes to court with all its expensive legal talent. It files suit. And sometimes our recommendation is overruled.[33]

In Korea, a different kind of problem arose recently when it was discovered that totally bogus products were being sold. For example, pills supposedly containing a life-and-death drug for severe heart disease were found to contain only flour. Government officials were so angered that they demanded a new law to punish those "who knowingly market a drug or food product which may cause human injury or death." The proposed punishment: death by hanging.[34]

The marketing and promotional practices of both multinational and domestic drug companies in capitalist and socialist countries alike can scarcely be denied. Few industry leaders have even attempted to deny them. Particularly in the United States, it is our feeling that, since the mid-1970s, a few important companies—a very few—have slowly and quietly begun to do things differently. They are telling the truth, the whole truth, and nothing but the truth. In every country in which they operate, they are saying essentially the same things to physicians about their products—a policy that means they are following FDA guidelines throughout the world. If unsuspected side effects appear and the company is required to remove a drug from the market in one country, it more or less promptly removes it from the market in all countries.

But although it seems that most companies do not deny the charges brought by critics, they continue to defend them. The defense mechanisms have become familiar:[35]

We do not need to tell physicians about the possible dangerous side effects. They are already aware of them. Medical experts and medical educators have bitterly denounced such a view. One distinguished hematologist in Mexico termed it "not merely nonsense but damnably dangerous nonsense."[36]

We do not need to list the warnings in the label. Our detail men or company reps are the ones to explain these to physicians. But in the Third World as well as in industrialized countries, salesmen are not often eager to knock their own products.

If the physician wants more data, all he has to do is write us a letter and ask for complete information. This could be a useful procedure, but few overworked physicians have the time to send in a query, and there is no guarantee that the company literature they receive will be unbiased.

We have no responsibility for the misuse of our products. The drug can be obtained only on a doctor's prescription. It's the doctor's responsibility. Such an argument possessed considerable persuasion until it became obvious that the "by prescription only" laws throughout Latin America, Africa, and Asia are uniformly ignored: virtually any prescription drug can be obtained without a prescription.

The differences between what we tell physicians in the United States and what we say in the Third World represent merely honest differences in opinion between honest scientists. Such a situation might hold in the case of a company seeking FDA approval to promote a particular product for the treatment of, say, acne or athlete's foot in the United States, a product that was refused approval because FDA ruled that the company's evidence was not convincing. The company, however, arguing that its evidence was convincing to its own scientists, proceeded to market the drug outside of the United States for acne and athlete's foot. This might well be an honest difference of opinion between honest scientists. But the argument becomes less palatable when it is found that the company promotes the product for acne and athlete's foot in Mexico, for only acne in the Philippines, for only athlete's foot in Kenya, and for a dozen totally different conditions in a dozen other countries.

But things are different in the Third World. This argument continues to baffle us. Does it mean that, south of the Rio Grande, east of Suez, and south of the Mediterranean, life is cheaper? That social responsibility doesn't matter?

We give complete information on our products to the drug regulatory agency in each country, and it is the responsibility of that agency to distribute as much or as little of that information to its health professionals as it wants.

It is probably true that most companies provide such material to the various governments, although the reliability of the information may sometimes be questionable. The second part of this defense, however, callously disregards the facts of life in the Third World. Governmental agencies may or may not have the legal or moral responsibility to disseminate this kind of information to physicians, pharmacists, nurses, and physician aides, but rarely if ever in developing countries do they have the money, the manpower, and the facilities to undertake an adequate job of dissemination.

Full information on our products is presented in package inserts or data sheets which are distributed along with the product or are sent to physicians who request them. Such a defense has been impressively reassuring in corporate headquarters and at stockholder meetings. In the real Third World, it is essentially meaningless. Package inserts, usually one sheet for each product, may well present in detail—sometimes in excessive detail—the recommendations for use and all or most of the known contraindications, warnings, precautions, and potential adverse reactions. Unfortunately, these sheets have been found to be virtually impossible to keep on file in a physician's office so that the information on perhaps several thousand products is quickly and easily available for examination. Keeping them up-to-date is difficult. Accordingly, they are infrequently used except by a few drug experts. Rarely if ever do they reach the nurses and physician aides outside of the big cities who have the responsibility of caring for the overwhelming majority of patients. What are used are the publications like *MIMS Africa, IIMS, DIMS,* and *PIMS,* which are convenient and relatively easy to use and are updated several times each year. They are found in the offices of almost every physician. Their pages are often dog-eared, with key sentences underlined in pencil or ink and handwritten notes in the margins. They are used. They represent probably the most important line of communication between drug company and physician, and the reliability and adequacy of this material is of unsurpassed importance.

A drug company has no control over what is printed about its products. We send the information to the publishers, and the editors change it any way they want. The impact of editorial policy is becoming apparent in a few cases. Thus, as was noted in the previous chapter, all entries for chloramphenicol products in *MIMS Africa* include a warning against use in trivial infections. In the same way, there seems to be a tendency for descriptions of diazepam (Valium) and related tranquilizers to include a warning that patients using such products should not take alcohol. But the publishers of the various drug compendia insist that they make relatively few important changes in the material sent in by the companies, and that these changes are submitted to each company for approval.

Some industry spokesmen, apparently seeking a scapegoat to blame for their heavily criticized labeling and promotion statements in *MIMS UK, MIMS Africa, IIMS,* and similar works, have expressed their general unhappiness with the editorial format and the editorial policies of these publications. The books, they say, provide inadequate space for adequate descriptions of the drug products. There is no room, they insist, to list the potential hazards (although it is obvious from our findings that some companies manage to find enough space for such information). In addition, the industry emphasizes that the *MIMS* publications cannot be regarded as suitable substitutes for detailed package inserts or product data sheets, such as those distributed routinely to physicians in the United States and Great Britain. But, as was noted above, in many if not most Third World countries, data sheets rarely go any farther than some office in the health ministry. They reach practicing physicians only infrequently. They are generally not used by health professionals in the field, mainly because there is no adequate system of distribution. In contrast, the *MIMS* books *are* widely distributed, and they *are* read. The defense that the industry does not approve of the policies of these publications is thus irrelevant.

It is much as if one would prefer to communicate by means of telephone, telegraph, or airmail, but the only available form of communication is carrier pigeons. Under such circumstances, one uses carrier pigeons.

The drug regulatory agency in each country tells us which claims may or may not be made, and which hazards must or must not be disclosed. This argument has been used with increasing frequency in recent years. It, too, has furnished reassurance in corporate headquarters. But, with only a few exceptions, it is simply not true. In some Latin American countries, especially since the mid-1970s, there has been mounting government pressure on drug companies to disclose the more important dangers inherent in their products. Some companies have improved their promotion and labeling in Latin America, but others have not. It is not clear whether this improvement is the result of governmental pressure or the decision by individual companies to accept their social responsibilities. In Africa and Asia, however, if there are effective government policies controlling drug labeling, these are not readily apparent. For example, as was noted in chapter 2, about half of the many dipyrone products listed for Indonesia carry clear warnings of the risk of agranulocytosis, while the others carry no warnings. Of the two dozen or so chloramphenicol products listed for the Philippines, about two-thirds carry more or less adequate warnings, while the others carry no warnings of any kind.

We market different products in developing countries because this is dictated by the different health conditions in those areas. Where such essentially exotic diseases as African sleeping sickness, hookworm, kala azar, and Chagas' disease are concerned, the defense is valid. But in the care of such common conditions as coughs, colds, pneumonia, tuberculosis, sinus infections, arthritis, syphilis, and staphylococeal and streptococcal infections, the argument is without much merit; these ailments can usually be treated effectively by products approved after extensive testing and already accepted for use in industrialized countries, and generally available at relatively low cost.

Although the industry accepts no blame for the widespread use of products like tonics and appetite stimulants, insisting it is merely meeting a demand, it was largely the industry which, through its advertising, its promotion, and its system of commissions, kickbacks, and gifts, created that demand in the first place.

No matter what you think, we're obeying the laws. Invoked as the industry's supposedly clinching argument, this defense once carried considerable weight in congressional hearings, stockholders meetings, and press conferences. It has less influence now. As we reported on Latin America, a number of nations have no national laws governing drug promotion. Thus, in those countries, a company that says "we're breaking no laws" is saying essentially, "we're breaking no laws that don't exist." But there are several Latin American countries—Colombia, El Salvador, Honduras, and Panama, in particular—that do have rules requiring the disclosure of hazards and contraindications. Those laws may not be enforced, but they are on the books. They are being blatantly violated. A drug company operating in those countries which does not disclose dangers and which still piously insists it is obeying the laws is, in fact, lying.

It now appears that there is a similar situation in the Third World countries of Africa and Asia: either no laws have been passed to control promotion or labeling, or the laws are apparently unenforced and perhaps unenforceable. In Nigeria, for example, the law bans the selling, labeling, or advertising of any drug in a way that is "false, or misleading, or is likely to create a wrong impression as to its quality, character, value, composition, merit, or safety." But government officials claim that the requirement is constantly and safely ignored.

Why has there been no attempt to enforce such laws? A Tanzanian official explains:

> The developing countries cannot afford to offend the Western powers. We depend on them for loans, for favorable trade agreements, for imports that are terribly important for us. If we are harsh on a British or an American company, perhaps the British or the American government will punish us.

During the past ten or twenty years, the multinationals have been increasingly accused of using people in the developing countries as guinea pigs. It has been claimed that if a new drug is tested in the Third World, and if it is found that it is effective and doesn't kill too many patients, the company will then request the approval of drug authorities to market the product in the United States and Europe. With a few but important exceptions—notably involving drugs developed for use only in the Third World—such charges are untrue. At least until the present time, regulatory agencies in the United States and other developed nations have seemed to be singularly unimpressed by the results of drug trials conducted on Third World populations. The industry appears to be well aware of this situation. Accordingly, patients in developing countries are generally viewed by the companies not as guinea pigs but simply as customers.

The recent furor over the marketing and promotion of infant-formula products in the Third World by Nestlé, American Home Products, and other multinational companies does not technically belong in a consideration of drug or food dumping. The infant-formula products have not been banned from the market in industrialized nations, where they fill a modestly important nutritional need. But the promotional techniques used by the manufacturers—strongly condemned by every member of the United Nations with only a single exception, the United States—are much like those of drug companies that conceal hazards, exaggerate claims, and dump dangerous drugs on poor countries.

A week after this country voted alone against the United Nations resolution, the San Francisco *Chronicle* published the following comment by its nationally famed, tongue-in-cheek columnist Arthur Hoppe:

As you know, the United States last week was the only country to vote against a U.N. resolution urging member states to curtail the promotion of artificial milk mixes for infants.

The World Health Organization estimated that one million babies in poor nations die each year as the result of their mothers being convinced that bottle feeding was far more "modern" and "scientific" than breast feeding.

Once the mother's own supply has dried up, the report said, she often runs out of funds to buy infant formula and her child dies of malnutrition. Or she mixes the powder with polluted water, and her child, who lacks the immunity provided by mother's milk, dies of a variety of diseases.

While all this may well be true, the Reagan administration countered with a telling argument against such emotional claptrap:

The U.N. resolution was in clear violation of the promotional rights of the $1.4 billion infant formula industry and a direct blow at the principles of the free enterprise system.

This is certainly true. The heart of the free enterprise system is a minimum of governmental controls on the producer and a maximum of freedom of choice for the customer.

So if a mother in Upper Volta chooses to starve or poison her child, it is surely her business and no concern of the busybody World Health Organization. Whose child is it, anyway?

Some critics worry that by causing one million deaths a year, the infant formula industry may be curtailing its market. Fortunately, this isn't true.

As luck would have it, the breast-feeding mother is unlikely to get pregnant while lactating and thus won't breed again for another year or two. The mother who employs the lethal bottle, on the other hand, can produce another offspring nine months after the birth of her first—thus assuring the industry a constant supply of hungry little customers.

This just shows you how the Good Lord smiles on the free enterprise system.

Let us also not forget that we are engaged in a battle for men's and women's minds. And say what you will for mother's milk, it doesn't do a thing for the free enterprise system. Breast feeding may be more healthful and more conducive to a warmer parent-child relationship. But it obviously instills in both mother and child the socialistic concept that there is, indeed, such a thing as a free lunch.

How far more rewarding is the life of the mother who labors 50 hours a week to earn the $28 a month it costs to buy formula for her infant. She must rest easier each night knowing she is contributing to the well being of the widows and orphans who own Nestlé's, Abbott Laboratories, Bristol Myers and American Home Products, Inc.

So enough of this U.N. interference in the free enterprise system. Let these do-gooders crack down instead on the uncivilized third world countries which produce the heroin, cocaine, and marijuana that are sapping the moral fiber of our American youth.

These unscrupulous dope pushers would do anything for a buck.[37]

5

BRIBERY AND OTHER STRATEGIES

Throughout the Third World, bribery and corruption reputedly represent an accepted way of life, a part of normal business practice. Of course such behavior is not limited to the Third World, as shall be seen below, and the companies who offer such bribes are surely no less culpable than the officials and physicians who accept them. The inducements are provided by—and sometimes demanded from—the drug companies, large and small, multinational and domestic, some based in the United States, Western Europe, and Japan, others based in communist-bloc nations. All of them are engaged in a fierce rivalry to win ever bigger markets for their products, or simply to maintain those markets. Where life-and-death drugs are concerned, getting them into the country and to the patients who need them desperately may be difficult without bribes. It may, in fact, be impossible.

"What we're doing is really not bribery," explains the head of an American drug company subsidiary in Malaysia. "When one of our company reps leaves a small gift a wall calendar, or a desk pad, or a fountain pen set—with a physician, it's merely to keep his friendship. We wouldn't want him to do anything wrong." Such small presents would probably have little influence on a physician's judgment in prescribing drugs.

Among the most effective of "small gifts" are free samples. In the United States, these are presumably intended to enable a physician to become familiar with a new product. In the Third World, they are intended to enable the physician to make more money. They are handed out in quantities of scores or hundreds of packages or bottles, often filling whole closets in a physician's office. For every ten containers the physician may order, for example, he will get two or three at no cost. There seems to be complete understanding that these free samples will be sold to patients, sometimes at the regular market price, often at a substantially higher price. Many of these free supplies are marked: *Free Sample, Not for Sale.* This warning apparently does not apply to sales by physicians or, in some instances, by pharmacists. It seems to mean that the *patient* is not supposed to sell them.

Another gambit widely employed, in industrialized countries as well, is the company cocktail party for physicians, or the so-called hospitality suite. In the United States, with a few exceptions, drug companies have learned to use such promotion with restraint. In some Third World countries, the entertainment is no less than lavish. A Swedish doctor who served in the Kenyan Ministry of Health said:

> Until you've seen one of those sumptuous buffets at a hotel like the New Stanley, in Nairobi, you can't believe it. Tables perhaps a hundred feet long, loaded with food. Maybe lobster, or shrimp, or a dozen kinds of meat dishes, and fish and egg dishes, and hot specialties, and two dozen salads, or caviar—even Iranian caviar—aren't too important to a well-to-do physician, but they're damned impressive to the younger doctors. They seem to be convinced that any company able to put on a party like that *must* be selling very good products.[1]

A somewhat different variety of promotion has been found—and filmed for television[2]—in the Philippines. At a Ciba-Geigy seminar for physicians, the regional marketing manager of the company expressed his thanks to the physicians. "Please remember," he told them, "that Ciba-Geigy stands committed to your medical education."

There were educational aspects. The program included lectures and medical films. Also included were pornographic films.

"There are many doctors who are interested, especially in the provinces, to see pornographic films from time to time," a company representative explained. "They want something out of the ordinary."

A television reporter asked, "So it's a real atmosphere of good friends?"

"Yes, really good friends," he said. "A close tie between doctors and medical reps and the medical companies. . . . It really helps in selling the products."

There was also a reception, with attractive young ladies serving as hostesses. Instead of carrying name tags identifying them as Felicia,

Josefina, Alicia, or the like, they wore sashes carrying such names as Entero-Vioform, Butazolidin, and Tanderil. For important physicians, special entertainment was provided, a "visit during the night."

"Women?" the representative was asked.

"Yes, women," he replied.

"That's also very important for the personal relationships?"

"Yes," the detail man said, "to build a good rapport with the doctors."

One of our colleagues told us later, "As I understand it, they give the docs a choice between a set of ballpoint pens and a girl. It seems they usually have a lot of ballpoint pens left over."

Less colorful but far more practical is the common practice of paying a kickback—"commission" might be a more tactful term—for each prescription a physician writes for the products of a particular manufacturer. The appropriate amount can be determined by a company detail man, who visits the physician's office regularly and reviews patients' records, or who goes to a pharmacy and determines which physician is writing how many prescriptions for which drugs. Few devices could be more influential in inducing physicians to order the largest possible amounts for the most expensive products, especially for drugs that are not clinically necessary.

"The system must work," claims a health official in Nigeria. "How else can you explain the fact that something like 30 percent of our drug bill goes for vitamin combinations, appetite stimulants, and other really unneeded medicines?"

Still another effective "free gift" approach is made to selected physicians who are influential leaders of medical organizations, hospitals, or groups that buy drugs in large quantities. For such key individuals, the free gift is not a calendar or a desk pad. It may be the free Mercedes-Benz sedan, or help in buying a new home, or the providing of a "scholarship" so the physician's children can be educated in a top-notch American or European university. It can be the free color-television set, or a home air-conditioning unit, a new microscope, or a home refrigerator. It can be the free, all-expense tour whereby the physician and his wife can travel to the United States, Japan, or Europe to attend a medical convention, or to inspect the company's factory, or simply to visit medical schools or museums or night clubs.

"If you have any of the funds left when you return home," one Filipino physician was told, "don't bother to give it back. That would only make problems for the people in our accounting office. Just put it in your bank account." Other physicians in the Philippines have been invited to give the number of their bank account to the company so that an appropriate check "in four digits" could be deposited automatically at regular intervals."[3]

Several multinational companies have found it useful to maintain a corps of what are known as "contract physicians," supposedly reputable doctors who are paid not merely for the prescriptions they order but also for signing testimonials and other endorsements or for writing laudatory articles for some medical journal. It may be noted that similar practices were found in the United States, where drug companies hired what one critic described as "stables" of experts.[4]

In Indonesia, the head of a hospital told us:

> We had great need for a new ward in the hospital, but the government could find no money for us. Then, the representatives of this Japanese firm came to us and said that, if only we would buy our drugs from them, they would build the ward for us and equip it completely at their expense. We rejected their kind offer. But, sadly, we still need the ward.

Although it appears that most "free gifts" in Third World countries are proferred by the drug companies, some physicians are not above soliciting such bribes on their own. In Kenya, for instance, one memorable case involved a leading professor at a medical school who went to four different companies with a request that each provide him with full travel expenses for himself and his wife so they could attend a medical conference in Europe. Three of the four firms each agreed to pay the bribe. In Indonesia, another memorable instance concerned a physician who told an American company official, "It would be helpful if I could obtain a new car. But a new Mercedes is not necessary. A Toyota would be very nice."

All of these techniques, whether the company offers the bribe or the physician asks for it, have been repeatedly denounced as unethical and often illegal. "Using high-powered methods, such as gifts, books, travel to international congresses, and sometimes indulging in the dishonest practice of the 'kickback,' by which the prescribing physician gets a percentage of the cost of what he prescribes," Herat Gunaratne, director of WHO's regional office in India, declared recently, "some of the multinational companies are exploiting the developing countries."[5]

Occasionally, drug company spokesmen have themselves viewed such practices with some degree of alarm and admitted their occurrence—which could scarcely be denied—but insisted that such occurrences were rare. "You don't damn the whole industry for just one or two rotten apples." But Segun Bambgose of the University of Lagos said to us, "We would estimate that, here in Nigeria, perhaps one-third of the total wholesale cost of all prescription drugs goes for bribes, or graft, or whatever you wish to call it. And in other parts of Africa, the situation may be even worse."[6] That might suggest a rather large proportion of rotten apples.

Somewhat similar types of corruption may be involved in negotiating with government agencies, either to win official approval for a new drug or to capture a particularly tempting contract. "But this is not really corruption," explains a company representative. "It is an accepted way of dealing with government officials. It merely lubricates the procedure."

In various Latin American countries, experts suggest that only small sums of money are paid, perhaps a few pesos given to some minor, underpaid government inspector to induce him "to look the other way." In some nations that technically require inspection of all imported drug products, it is possible, on the payment of a relatively modest amount, to obtain a "waiver of inspection." Such a waiver, it is held, does not make it possible to import defective products; rather, "it speeds up the business, so that you get approval in a few hours instead of a few months."

In other negotiations, more substantial payments—in the tens or even hundreds of thousands of dollars—may be at stake. An East African journalist says:

> Here there is usually a most-favored company. It may be a local, domestic company that has been wise enough to put the wife or son-in-law of a top government official on its board of directors. Or it may be one of the big multinationals that is hungry for business. Usually, even before there is an invitation for bids, knowledgeable people know who will get the contract.

Experts point out that the low bid, even from the most reputable American and European companies, does not always win acceptance.

One of the more unhappy aspects of such "lubricating of the procedure" has been the purchase of some drugs in remarkably large quantities. In 1973, for example, two officials of the Ministry of Health in Kenya were jailed for accepting bribes of 100,000 shillings (about $14,000) for ordering for government use what were termed enormous quantities of drugs, including enough Valium to last the country for ten years and enough of an antibacterial agent, Bactrim, to last for thirteen years. Both drugs were produced by Hoffmann-La Roche. In the newspaper accounts, however, the Swiss firm was not identified.[7]

In Tanzania, John Yudkin found that the government's Central Medical Stores contained these stocks:

— a 5.3-year supply of Penbritin capsules (ampicillin), a 6.4-year supply of Orbenin capsules (cloxacillin), and a 10.7-year supply of Parentrovite (a high-potency combination vitamin product), all made by the British firm Beecham;

— an 8.3-year supply of Ketrax (a remedy for intestinal worms) from Imperial Chemical Industries in England;

— a 22.0-year supply of Endoxan (an antitumor agent) and a 38.0-year supply of Avamigran (an antimigraine product), both made by Asta-Werke in West Germany;

— an 8.5-year supply of Lasix (a diuretic), a 13.0-year supply of Jonit (a remedy for hookworm), and a 46.0-year supply of Reverin (an injectable tetracycline product), all marketed by the West German firm Hoechst.

There was also more than a 5-year supply of a slow-acting form of insulin known as lente insulin. No manufacturer was indicated. Yudkin wrote:

> It is not possible to define the reasons why such overpurchasing has occurred. There is no direct evidence of corruption or bribery. For some drugs, it may be sensible to buy large stocks. Other drugs, however, have a limited shelf life, and if overpurchased they either will have to be consumed in large amounts or will expire and have to be discarded.[8]

The shelf life of such products as antibiotics and insulin is generally supposed to be two or three years in temperate climates. In the tropical climate of Tanzania, the shelf life may be less than half that long. Although physicians were urged to use up the overstocked products before expiration of their shelf life, an estimated $1 million worth had to be destroyed, representing not only a waste of drugs but a tragic waste of the country's meager supply of funds.

It seems noteworthy that, in all affairs of this sort, the company—especially if it is an important multinational company—is virtually never punished. "Bribery is a two-way street," says a drug expert in East Africa. "If there is a bribe-taker, there must obviously be a bribe-giver. But we never accuse the bribe-giver, at least in public. We cannot afford to antagonize the Western companies."

Efforts to keep from offending the powerful companies in Europe and the United States have sometimes been exceedingly curious. In Tanzania, for example, two English physicians working at the University of Dar es Salaam—one of the most distinguished in East Africa—prepared a report for presentation at a scientific meeting on the hazards of dipyrone and chemically related analgesics. They had apparently failed to foresee how these comments might upset several European drug companies that were marketing such drugs all over Africa as remedies for headache, neuralgia, toothache, menstrual pain, and similar conditions. Just before the conference, university officials were told by the embassy of one country that "such criticism might be inadvisable" at a time when that country was funding a major aid program for Tanzania, in this instance helping to finance a new building for the university's engineering college. Under pressure from university officials, the physicians agreed to withdraw their paper.[9]

In these attempts to buy a physician's friendship—or at least his orders—domestic companies in India, East Africa, Indonesia, and the Philippines are reportedly at least as active as the multinational firms. The head of a Philippine company claims:

> We are forced to do this. We must get business. Unless we offer more attractive commissions, we cannot compete with the big foreign firms. We have products of good quality, and our prices are reasonable, but we do not have their famous reputations.

Since the late 1970s American drug companies have been less involved, especially where bribes and similar inducements to government officials are concerned. Such inducements to officials could scarcely be dismissed as trivial. In 1976, twenty-two U.S. manufacturers of drugs and similar health products reported making more than $31.4 million in what were described as "questionable overseas payments."[10] Most of these were made to officials in government or regulatory agencies. Since about 1977, however, this kind of bribery by U.S. firms has been markedly reduced. There is no evidence that this change has been the result of a sudden outbreak of acute virtue among the companies. Most attribute it to the Lockheed, Gulf Oil, Northrop, and similar scandals and the resultant passage by Congress of the 1977 Foreign Corrupt Practices Act, which outlaws bribes to foreign government officials. The Act unquestionably makes it more difficult to have bribery payments accepted as a normal business expense for tax purposes. Under the new law, bribing an individual physician who, because of the scarcity of doctors in a Third World country, may be able to dictate the drug use of 10,000 or 15,000 or 20,000 patients, may be unethical, but nonetheless legal, while offering a similar bribe to a government bureaucrat is illegal. "Furthermore," claims a top official of a New Jersey-based drug company, "if one of my salesmen is caught giving a special little present to some health ministry man, in, say, Africa, or India, or Korea—why, hell, they might fine my company a million dollars and put *me* in jail for five years!"

Many American drug firms insist that they have been significantly harmed by the new policy. "They tell me they are hurting," says Dal-Hyun Chi, head of pharmaceutical affairs in Korea's Health Ministry. "They complain that they are losing business to their Japanese and European competitors, and even to some Korean firms that are entering the world market. I believe them."[11]

By the spring of 1981, with the new Reagan administration in power, there were signs that relief might be in sight for the beleaguered American companies and that "little bribes" should be viewed more tolerantly. In an interview with the Chicago *Tribune,* Secretary of Commerce Malcolm Baldrige asserted that small "facilitating payments" to foreign officials are not really bribes. "That's something called 'grease,'" he said. "It's sometimes called 'facilitating payments,' but it means you are not trying to bribe anybody to do anything outside of the law, or changing their payment, or buying your product."[12] The *Wall Street Journal* greeted the prospects with an article headlined "U.S. Business Overseas: Back to Bribery?"[13]

In most of Africa, Asia, and Latin America, the practice of bribery by a drug company, whether to a physician or to someone in a government agency, is hardly a hush-hush matter. It is discussed openly at dinner parties and legislative hearings. Occasionally, it breaks out in a rash of newspaper exposés, but usually it creates little excitement. Unless the affair is blatant, no one goes to jail or is even chastized. As an Indian customs official explained it a few years ago, "When you take a bribe, the only danger is if you forget to share it with your superior."

One storm has raged publicly for years over the head of Arsenio Regala, the controversial administrator of the Food and Drugs Administration in the Philippines. Critics have frequently claimed that his modest government salary could not conceivably enable him to afford his life style, his home (described as "wall-to-wall luxury"), and an expensive American college education for his son. "Of course, I have been accused of taking bribes," he freely admits. "But this is because I am a chemist, not a pharmacist." His wife, who *is* a pharmacist, heads the FDA bureau that is responsible for approving and registering new drug products, "It is simply that some people are jealous of me. Of course, I have never accepted any bribe of any kind."[14]

It is one thing if the bribe, the commission or kickback, or other skulduggery means that the physician will prescribe a drug which is more costly than another but which is just as safe and just as effective. Such an act may represent a waste of money which the patient or the government can ill afford to lose, but presumably it will not cause any clinical damage. It is totally different if the outcome of bribery may result in injury or death—if the prescribed drug is unsafe, ineffective, contaminated, adulterated, likely to spoil soon in storage, needlessly complicated, or if the patient's or the government's few dollars are allocated not to urgently needed and often life-and-death products but frittered away on such pharmaceuticals as tonics, appetite stimulants, costly vitamin combinations, and other low-priority frills.

Probably the greatest danger in drug bribery lies in its effect on national drug policies. One distinguished drug expert says:

> Every time we try to improve our policies here, every time we try to establish a really effective drug regulatory system, to increase the use of low-cost, high-quality generic products, to get the necessary laws passed and enforced, to require all drug companies to tell doctors all the truth about their products, we are blocked. Most of this opposition comes from high-ranking physicians in the hospitals and the medical societies who are commonly understood to be taking bribes. They have been bought by the big brand-name companies.

In industrialized nations, apparently few people were aware of the extent of drug bribery, and most of them comforted themselves with the belief that such bribery might be regrettable, but, fortunately, it involved only the poorer countries of the Third World. In 1981, this consoling idea was rudely shattered. A four-man Austrian team reported that essentially the same kinds of bribery and corruption were going on in such scarcely underdeveloped countries as Austria, Switzerland, and West Germany.[15]

Two members of the investigative team were award-winning reporters for newspapers, radio, and television. One, also a writer, was a trained psychologist. The fourth, writing under an assumed name, was (but no longer remains) a drug company official. It was this official who, disgusted by the practices he had observed in the drug industry, coached the psychologist-reporter so he could obtain a job as drug company detail man, or representative. In a short time, the team managed to "liberate" some 40,000 documents, many of them confidential, including interoffice memoranda, reports on detailer visits to physicians, and physician requests for donations. Among the companies involved were Bayer in Germany, Sandoz in Switzerland, and Aesca, an Austrian representative of U.S.-based Schering.

> As in the Third World, physicians—especially dispensing physicians who sold drugs to their own patients—were greedy for free samples. "Professional conversations during visits to doctors' offices scarcely exist. ... The doctors become increasingly bolder and preoccupied with demands for gifts."
>
> At medical conventions, physicians come equipped with large shopping bags as they visit each exhibit. At one company exhibit, the company may limit the amount of free samples to 2,000 Austrian schillings (about $120) for each physician. But there may be as many as a hundred such exhibits at the convention, and an individual doctor can take home $12,000 worth of free drugs, which he will sell to his patients.
>
> "What are we doing here but distributing free gifts?" an exhibit attendant complained. "Our activity here is merely corruption."
>
> Free samples play a prominent role in what are termed "continuing education evenings." One indignant elderly physician described such a program in these words: "The seventy physicians and their spouses arrive. There is a short film, a lecture, and then the main event, the big feast. ... Late at night, you see drunken physicians and their wives leave with full plastic bags in both hands. This is senseless. ... I am close to retirement and old enough to dare say such a thing."
>
> Free trips also have their value, and physicians and their wives are given—or ask for—travel funds in order to visit Corfu, or London, or New York, or San Francisco.

One company used an Airbus and three chartered Lufthansa Boeing 727s to take seven hundred German physicians and their wives to a four-day "seminar" on the Greek Island of Rhodes. There were side trips to the scenic beauties of Rhodes, barbecues with grilled specialties, a buffet with typical hot and cold Greek dishes at the covered swimming pool, wine by the barrel, a fur fashion show, cocktails in the garden, and a gala dinner. There was a scientific meeting each day, but "there were seldom more than a small part of the doctors to be seen there."

One official of an Austrian hospital expressed his thanks to Bayer for sending him to visit England, and added, "Further preference and purchase of your firm's products in the hospital is to be understood."

A physician at the University Medical Clinic in Graz wrote, "I dare already now to thank you for your help and assure you that also I will use your products in the future."

In the case of an Austrian physician who was about to decide whether to use Carlo Erba Farmitalia's costly antibiotic Tetralysal or the less expensive Achromycin from Lederle, a detail man told his superiors, "There is a possibility he will keep on using Tetralysal if we send for his department this year 10,000 Austrian schillings."

Many top physicians and clinic directors, it was disclosed, accept funds sent to their institutions for medical research, but often they request that the "research" funds be sent directly to their accounts in a foreign bank.

Each company, the investigators found, keeps on file the reports from each detailer on every visit he makes to a physician. Among the questions which the company representative is supposed to answer about each physician are these:

—What are his personal habits?

—Does he have a big practice?

—How does he stand with our competitors?

—Is he a "sample hunter"?

—Is he a good businessman?

—Which gifts and contributions has he already received?

—Is his office help pretty?

—Is he bribable?

—Where does he go on vacation, and with whom?

One company representative reported—with obvious amazement—that an Austrian physician had "gone on vacation to Crete *with his own wife!*"

In the case of physicians who criticize or attack a particular product, the investigators said, companies have hired detectives to "explore the private life and family relations of the critical doctors."

One of the Austrian investigators described a meeting of Bayer detail men who were warned by a company official to maintain secrecy. "I beg you, gentlemen," he said, "please think of the fact that you have a lot of information in your hands that is confidential and that concerns no one outside of our group. I don't mean by that only our competitors, but also reporters."

One member of the audience was not visibly impressed. Although present as a detail man, he was actually a reporter member of the investigative team. Afterwards, the reporter wrote in his notes. "With great difficulty, I suppress a smile. I have found out enough about the practices of Bayer. A few days later, I hand in my resignation."

There was apparently no reason to believe that the activities noted in this investigation were substantially different from the performances of other companies.

In the Austrian study, it was reported that the bribes to physicians were usually modest in size, usually between 20,000 and 50,000 schillings, or between $1,200 and $3,000 per company. The physicians were not merely for sale; they were for sale at bargain prices. So much for the Hippocratic oath and the doctor's pledge to avoid corruption.

"If this kind of thing happens in countries like Austria and Germany and Switzerland," says Olle Hansson of the University of Göteborg, "how can anyone doubt that it goes on in the developing countries?"

Those who have had long experience working in Third World countries feel that it will be difficult to halt or even minimize bribery in those nations. Bribery is and possibly always will be an accepted way of life. It is not restricted to the drug industry, but seems to be involved in everything from buying and selling telecommunications and office equipment, school supplies, whiskey, and warplanes to winning a contract to build a highway or a hydroelectric plant, or even to getting a bank loan. But in the case of drugs, with all their potential to heal and to harm, bribery may be not only a way of life—it may be a way of death.

6

THE OPTIONS

Spokesmen for the drug industry have long and insistently proclaimed that rigid and complex drug regulatory systems like those established by the U.S. Food and Drug Administration are needlessly time-consuming, costly, irksome, and—most of all—unnecessary. There may have been some unfortunate occurrences in the past, they admit, but this can never happen again. The companies, the spokesmen say, now recognize their responsibilities to society and will live up to them, with or without government regulation.

The validity of such a guarantee can be tested. How do the companies behave in countries like the United States and Great Britain, where regulatory agencies are tough and effective? How do the same companies perform in Africa, Asia, and Latin America, where drug regulation is weak or nonexistent?

Such a comparison does not build up great confidence in the willingness or the ability of the drug industry to police itself. As we have shown in earlier chapters of this book, the promotion of drugs in the Third World by most companies—though certainly not all of them—is marked by puffed-up claims of effectiveness which cannot be supported by substantial scientific evidence. In this promotion, contraindications

Some of the issues discussed here are considered in greater depth in such important works as the following: Richard Blum, Andrew Herxheimer, Catherine Stenzl, and Jasper Woodcock (eds.), *Pharmaceuticals and Health Policy: International Perspectives on Provision and Control of Medicines* (London: Croom Helm, 1981); Orville L. Freeman, *The Multinational Company: Instrument for World Growth* (New York: Praeger Publishers, 1981); and Vicente Navarro (ed.), *Imperialism, Health and Medicine* (Farmingdale, New York: Baywood, 1981).

131

and potentially serious or lethal adverse reactions are minimized, glossed over, or totally omitted. Essential warnings, sometimes life-and-death warnings, are not consistently given to physicians and pharmacists.

(In the United States, most industry leaders have not gone along with attempts to dump FDA. Privately, they say they not only can live with ·FDA but probably could not live without it. If FDA were abolished, or its legal authority seriously weakened, their companies would be no match for their less responsible competitors.)

The record of drug industry performance in the developing countries shows still other blemishes. Drugs banned from the market in industrialized nations as ineffective or excessively dangerous are dumped on poorer nations. Needless "luxury" products—all of them expensive and most of them of minimal clinical importance—are flooded onto the market and promoted by costly but effective sales campaigns. Prices for identical products in the Third World are often set far higher than those listed in the United States and Europe. Indira Gandhi, Prime Minister of India, told a 1981 meeting of the World Health Assembly: "Medicines which may be of the utmost value to poorer countries can be bought by us only at exorbitant prices."[1] Bribery and corruption by industry of both physicians and government officials are accepted and sometimes sought after.

So far as the more than five hundred drug products in our studies are concerned, there would appear to be no substantial differences in the performances of multinational companies, domestic companies, brand-name companies, generic-name companies, companies based in capitalistic nations, and companies based in socialistic or communist-bloc nations. On the basis of the products concerned in this analysis, the Third World promotion and labeling presented by many firms based in the United States and the United Kingdom cannot be accepted as adequately truthful, complete, and scientifically sound. It is our impression, however, that U.S. and British promotion is more responsible than that used by many multinational companies based in West Germany, Switzerland, and other industrialized nations. It is also our impression that the promotion presented by most multinational companies is more reliable than that presented by domestic firms based in the developing countries themselves. Whether such findings would hold for all products marketed by all companies is impossible to predict.

The results of irresponsible promotional practices in developing countries are tragic: the wastage of scarce funds on luxury drugs, the failure to buy low-cost generic products of high quality, horrendous drug shortages, and most tragic, needless injury and death.

The industry sees itself as relatively free of any wrong-doing. Claudia Baskin of the Pharmaceutical Manufacturers Association said early in 1981 that "most of the U.S. industry has little to apologize for in the realm of 'social responsibility' and the pharmaceutical industry least of all."[2]

Such a view scarcely jibes with that of Halfdan Mahler, Director-General of the World Health Organization, who denounced the activities of multinational drug companies in the Third World as "drug colonialism" and described their performance as "indecency."[3] Baskin's view is not supported by the data presented in this book (see chapter 2) nor by those presented earlier on the performance of United States firms in Latin America.[4] More recently, however, some U.S.-based companies appear to have done a more responsible job of drug promotion.

George Teeling-Smith, long accepted as an authority on the British pharmaceutical industry, has suggested that critics of the companies may be expecting too much. He said:

> You must understand the reason multinational companies try to grab back as much profit as possible out of the less developed countries is frankly because they are suspicious of the future stability of their operations there. I would just be talking rubbish if I were to say that the multinational companies were operating in the less developed countries for the welfare of those countries. They are not bishops, they are businessmen.[5]

A wide variety of solutions for the problem have been proposed. Some of these would appear to be totally unrealistic. Wiping out bribery of physicians and government officials, or even reducing corruption by any substantial degree, will probably not be readily accomplished. The mere enactment of new laws or regulations in the Third World cannot have any value unless they can be enforced. Unfortunately, enforcement is itself an expensive maneuver; regulators and inspectors would have to be employed, and—with the small salaries paid to government workers in developing countries—the inspectors themselves could be easily bribed.

More serious attention has been directed toward other approaches which have been considered, sometimes superficially and sometimes in great depth, in a rapidly mounting number of studies. These have touched on such areas as improved drug production, quality control, labeling, formularies, and pricing. Beginning in the mid-1970s, many of the important investigations and developments have been undertaken by the World Health Organization and such agencies of the United Nations as UNCTAD (the United Nations Conference on Trade and Development), UNIDO (the United Nations Industrial Development Organization), and UNICEF (the United Nations Children's Fund). A review of the actions and reports of these and related groups has recently been published.[6] In the United States, a number of aspects that are now of international importance were examined even earlier, in the late 1960s, by the Task Force on Prescription Drugs of the Department of Health, Education, and Welfare (now Health and Human Services), at the request of the President.[7]

More recently, in 1979, the Institute of Medicine/National Academy of Sciences studied the situation at the request of the Congress.[8] Many other studies have been conducted by various individuals or organizations in this country, Great Britain, Europe, and many of the developing countries themselves.

There are a number of options for action which deserve careful consideration by government agencies, national and international, and by consumer groups, medical and pharmacy organizations, drug experts, economists, and the drug industry. What may be of tremendous importance is the atmosphere in which these and related matters are analyzed, discussed, and debated. We would hope that the drug issues could be examined as drug issues. But there is a real danger, we feel, that the study could degenerate into another noisy, hemorrhagic confrontation of capitalism and socialism, with matters of political economy totally overshadowing pharmacological and pharmaceutical realities.

Such ineffective confrontations have already taken place. The products manufactured in a socialist country like Poland are dismissed as inferior because they are socialist products. Multinational companies are attacked, not because they are profit-making firms which are doing evil things, but because they are profit-making, or simply because they are multinational. (Whether making a profit of any kind is evil in itself is yet to be adequately demonstrated. And if operating internationally is inherently bad, then something should be done about the World Bank, the Boy Scouts, and the International Red Cross.) The views expressed by a pharmacologist of unquestioned competence are ignored because he is in favor of socialism, or because he is opposed to it. American firms are assailed because they are American, Japanese firms because they are Japanese, and British firms because they are British. Depending on the circumstances, such terms as formulary, government regulation, patents, profits, and free enterprise are supposedly not for use in polite society.

In this connection, it should be noted that the use of all-encompassing attacks or all-encompassing denials is associated with grave risks. The blanket denials of any wrongdoing by the American drug industry, especially during the 1960s, resulted in a disastrous loss of credibility. The current across-the-board denunciation of all multinational companies by consumer activist groups may well lose these groups their most valuable weapon, their credibility in the eyes of the public.

COUNTRY-OF-ORIGIN RULE

Among the methods which have been given considerable attention is the so-called country-of-origin rule. Under this concept, no drug could be marketed in any nation, developed or developing, unless it is approved for use in the country of origin, the country in which it is manufactured. It has been optimistically presumed that such a procedure would effectively stop the practice of drug-dumping. If a drug were banned as unsafe in the United States or Great Britain, for example, it could not be marketed in the Third World by any American or British firm.

In our view, the country-of-origin rule would be impractical for one simple reason: it could be a hoax. It could be readily evaded by what might be called the South Slobovian Connection.

Consider a hypothetical American drug company, Zilch Laboratories, which has developed a new antibiotic, Zilchomycin. Unfortunately for the company, Zilchomycin was rejected by FDA on the grounds that it is unsafe. Therefore, it cannot be marketed in this country. Does this block the company from selling Zilchomycin to a Third World country with a country-of-origin rule? It does not. It means that the company will simply need to find another country, which we are calling South Slobovia, and there build a small manufacturing plant. If the requisite inducement is paid to cooperative drug officials in South Slobovia, the product will be approved for use in that country, and South Slobovia becomes the "country of origin." Thereafter, Zilchomycin can be legally marketed throughout the Third World.

This is essentially what happened in the case of Upjohn's 90-day injectable contraceptive Depo-Provera, which was not approved for use as a contraceptive in the United States but was manufactured and approved—without any need for bribing anyone—in Belgium. The Belgian drug-regulatory program is one of the best in Europe. Depo-Provera is now accepted for use as a contraceptive in most western European countries and widely in the Third World. But if South Slobovia were a country without a rigorous drug-regulatory system, the risk to patients could be enormous.

It is our considered belief that no country-of-origin regulation should be adopted unless the exporting country had a well-established record of requiring adequate evidence of safety and efficacy—countries such as the United States, Great Britain, the Netherlands, Norway, and Sweden.

As one corollary, it has been proposed that the United States Congress pass some kind of law making it illegal for any American company to market any unapproved drug, even if it were actually manufactured outside of the United States, in any country in the world. Such a law would probably be unconstitutional and almost certainly unenforceable.

As another approach, it has been suggested that the United States law be changed to permit the export of unapproved drugs under conditions that would meet the special needs of Third World countries and, at the same time, provide protection to the people of the developing nations. Thus, the Secretary of Health and Human Services would have to find that the product was requested and approved by the importing country, that the health officials of the importing country had been fully informed of all known indications and hazards of the drug, that the drug would not represent any significant risk to health in the importing country, and that the arrangement was "appropriate." Such a procedure is now permitted in this country for the export of medical devices.

CERTIFICATION OF IMPORTED DRUGS

As a somewhat related step in protecting the people of developing countries from unsafe, ineffective, or otherwise unapproved products manufactured overseas, WHO has attempted to establish what is known as the certification scheme for pharmaceutical products moving in international commerce. It would require the appropriate governmental agency, usually the Ministry of Health or a comparable department, in the exporting country to certify to the government of the importing country that the product has been approved for marketing, or, if not, why not. On the basis of such information, the importing country could decide whether or not to accept the product.

Such an approach would be broader than the country-of-origin rule, since it would provide Third World countries with information on drugs not approved or disapproved in the country of manufacture. This method has been endorsed by the health agencies in many if not most industrialized countries. In the developing countries, however, perhaps as the result of industry pressure applied locally on the health authorities, it has not yet received wide support.

LOCAL PRODUCTION

In the opinion of some, the only long-term solution to the problem— providing the Third World with relatively safe, effective, low-cost drug products that are honestly and accurately labeled and promoted—would be to enable the developing nations to produce and distribute the products themselves. While such production might well improve the availability of low-cost products, any arguments that this in itself would lead to more honest and accurate labeling do not seem to be persuasive.

There do not appear to be any serious barriers to prevent a developing country with adequate resources from taking on the last stage of production, that is, purchasing the finished chemicals on the open market and then putting them into final dosage form as capsules, tablets, or solutions.

To undertake the more formidable task of producing the finished chemicals from raw materials is another matter, requiring complex and often expensive equipment, highly sophisticated technical knowledge, skilled manpower, and sizable investment. So far, only four Third World countries have developed important local private or government drug industries: Mexico, Brazil, India, and Cuba.[9] (A drug industry is now being built in the People's Republic of China, but little detailed information is available.) Mexico and Brazil are filling significant portions of their own drug needs, and Indian firms are now exporting to other parts of the world. The Indian program, however, has been marked by serious difficulties, and, in recent years, nearly 20 percent of the drugs analyzed were found to be substandard.[10] The program in

Cuba appears to be far more successful. "In sharp contrast to the de-
pendence on imports for 70–80 percent of drug supplies in 1958, national production in 1978 satisfied 82 percent of the total requirements
of the country," an UNCTAD study reported. Further, Cuba is now
exporting a considerable number of important drug products to other
countries, not only in Latin America but also in Africa and Asia.[11]

A few other countries, notably Egypt and Argentina, appear to be well
started on developing local drug industries, and others may get into
significant production during the 1980s. But as a major factor in solving
the problems of drug supply, local production appears to have only
limited value for the foreseeable future. Few multinational companies
have shown much eagerness to share their technological knowledge with
the Third World, especially with countries in which their patented products have been pirated, their factories are threatened with government
seizure, they get what they consider to be minimal direct financial return
from the tropical-disease drugs they do market, and they are constantly
berated for not developing more agents to control tropical ailments. Harold Simon of the University of California in San Diego says:

> A company must choose how to devote scarce resources of space,
> trained personnel, and funds to research on drugs that may possibly
> work, and may possibly work in developing countries, instead of pursu-
> ing the much less risky development of second- or third-order derivatives
> of drugs already in use in the industrialized world. With some justifica-
> tion, the industry can ask why it should devote scarce resources to the
> development of new drugs when effective and cheap drugs are rotting in
> warehouses and never reach patients because of inadequate delivery sys-
> tems.[12]

On the other hand, an UNCTAD report charged that the pursuit of
private profit by the multinational drug companies "is not compatible
with the well-being of the vast majority of the world's population."[13]

It may be some time before the companies and their most outspoken
critics see eye to eye.

DRUG PATENTS

The abolition of all or most drug patents has been urged for many
years. It poses an exceedingly difficult question. Is it more important to
get rid of patents so that the scientific resources and technological skills

of the industrialized nations can be more equitably shared now with the Third World, or to preserve the patent system—with possibly some modifications—so that future generations can be able to control diseases that are today uncontrollable?

The question carries serious implications—ethical, clinical, economic, and most certainly political. No matter which answer is chosen, many millions of people will suffer. It seems to us that wiping out patent protection for new drugs would be a short-term boon for some countries but a long-term disaster for the world. It would effectively choke off much if not most of the industry's research and the development of better drugs. Some industry critics have countered that much of the industry's research is wasteful and needless, and that the important investigations can be taken over easily by university and government laboratories. For the last thirty or forty years, however, the record is clear that although some of these nonindustry institutions have contributed magnificently to basic research, they have turned out few important new products. Certainly in difficult economic times with tight budgets, few government agencies or university research centers would be willing to take the gamble of investing the enormous resources and the many years now required in modern drug development.

There are, of course, other things that can be done to the drug patent system. Some Third World countries have already found one solution: they simply ignore international patents. Some industrialized countries have required compulsory licensing after a reasonably brief period of monopoly. There could be a two-tier type of patent length: a long period of patent protection in industrialized countries and a short period in developing nations. Patents could be blocked on only "essential drugs." In this connection, it is important to note that few of the products on the WHO list of essential drugs are still covered by patent.

NATIONAL FORMULARIES

Unlike a drug compendium, which is a listing of all drugs—or all drugs of a particular class—legally on the market, a formulary is a listing of only those drugs recommended or approved for use in a particular hospital, a private health-insurance program, or a state or federal program. During the late 1960s, the idea of using a drug formulary in such programs as Medicaid and Medicare was bitterly assailed by the brand-name industry, especially if such a formulary would list drugs by their generic names.

Industry spokesmen insisted that such formularies would result in second-class health care, cause the companies to cut down on their research, be an intolerable interference with the right of a physician to prescribe as he saw fit, and probably be unconstitutional in the first place. The HEW Task Force on Prescription Drugs investigated the situation and came out with a different conclusion:

> In general, American physicians have found a formulary acceptable and practical, especially when it is designed by their clinical and scientific colleagues serving on expert committees, when quality is considered at least as important as price, when the formulary can be revised at appropriate intervals, and when there are provisions for prescribing unlisted drug products where special clinical conditions so demand. . . . The use of a formulary is not a mark of second-class medicine but is, in fact, associated with the provision of the highest quality of medicine in the outstanding hospitals in the Nation.[14]

The Task Force likewise found that it could not accept the claims by some brand-name firms that generic-name drugs were second-class products and could not be trusted.

> On the basis of available evidence, lack of clinical equivalency among chemical equivalents meeting all official standards has been grossly exaggerated as a major hazard to the public health.[15]

This conclusion was based on the situation as it was known in 1968. Since that time, few additional examples of *clinically* significant differences between brand- and generic-name products have turned up in the United States. Of these, probably the most important involved generic versions of digoxin, some marketed by brand-name firms and others by generic companies.

Since the Task Force's report was published in 1969 most drug companies have found they can live with a formulary system, especially if each hospital or each state has its own formulary. As one company official put it, "With many different formularies in existence, you may miss out on some but you'll win on others."

What alarmed the major firms in the United States was the chilling prospect that someday a single formulary, especially if it required rather than recommended compliance, might be established for the entire coun-

try. This could well nullify the enormous and enormously effective promotional campaigns staged by some companies: no matter how heavily a
product might be promoted, the campaign would be useless if the drug
were not accepted by the formulary committee.

By the mid-1970s, it was apparent that the development of national
formularies in some parts of the world could very well become a reality.
In Sri Lanka, a formulary of only a few hundred items seemed to be
working effectively, although to the intense discomfort of the multinational companies. In India, a government committee estimated that the
country's basic drug needs could be satisfied by "just 116 generic drugs,
less than 1 percent of the 15,000 branded drugs sold there at present."[16]
A government agency in Brazil which provides drugs free or at low cost
to the poor was dealing with only 108 generic products, of which 52
were classified as essential.[17]

Then came an even more frightening prospect for the multinational
companies—the possibility of an *international* formulary. In 1977, an
expert panel of the World Health Organization published what has
become known as the WHO list of essential drugs.[18] It proposed 214
products, of which 182 were classified as "essential" and 32 as "comple-
mentary." Few of these still had patent protection; for most, their patents had expired and they could be bought on the world market as
generics and probably at low cost. The list was not exactly a formulary.
It was put forth as suggested guidelines which could and probably
should be modified by each nation to fit its own medical and economic
situation. It certainly had no force of law. Nevertheless, it sent some
drug companies and their trade associations into a near panic.

The International Federation of Pharmaceutical Manufacturers Associations (IFPMA) warned: "An essential drugs list is, we believe,
faulty in both its medical and economic reasoning. Adoption of the
WHO report's recommendations . . . might well reduce health standards
already attained."[19]

A restricted prescribing list, said the Association of the British Pharmaceutical Industry, would "disastrously inhibit the development of future pharmaceutical innovation." This is the familiar "we'll be forced to
cut down on our research" threat, which has long since lost most of its
force in the United States but may maintain some brief credibility in
other parts of the world.

Another IFPMA statement declared, "It must be emphasized that any limited list will leave a certain part of the population's needs without adequate treatment and can thus by no means satisfy medical requirements."[20] This argument neatly skirted the unpleasant fact that an enormous part of the population in the Third World was *already* without adequate treatment. The list had been developed as an attempt to fill the gap.

In another denouncement, the president of IFPMA claimed that the concept was being strongly advocated by left-wing radicals in developed countries.[21] He was undoubtedly correct, but only in part. The concept was being advocated by left-wing radicals in the Third World, too, and also by some right-wingers and middle-of-the-roaders.

A slightly more temperate view was presented in a UNIDO report: "There is an entrenched hostility to reforms of this sort, not just from the transnational corporations whose activities would be curtailed by them, but also from many doctors, consumers, and people generally who believe in the free market."[22] The free enterprise system, it may seem, is not universally beloved.

The WHO essential-drugs list and others like it are intended not so much to reduce drug expenditures—which, in most developing countries, will almost certainly continue to be inadequate under any conditions—but to assure that available funds will be allocated to provide the maximum benefits to the maximum number of patients with the most serious, life-threatening, disabling diseases. Accordingly, whereas the list would provide minimal assistance to victims of such conditions as the common cold, the "flu," and minor skin irritations, it would make possible maximum help for those with malaria, typhoid fever, cholera, pneumonia, leprosy, and other serious or life-threatening diseases. Thus, noticeably absent from the list are duplicative antibiotics, combination drugs with few or no clinical advantages and some with disadvantages, costly vitamin combinations, tonics, irrational hormone mixtures, and most products previously banned in industrialized nations as unsafe or ineffective.

Proponents of the formulary approach for developing countries agree overwhelmingly on one point: *the objective is not to reduce total drug expenditures—which are already inadequate—but to reallocate these expenditures so that they will provide the greatest possible benefits to the most patients with the greatest needs for help.* Or, as one community health expert expressed it, "You don't fritter away your scarce money to buy drugs for hay fever when people are dying from cholera for lack of tetracycline."

The impact on any individual country which decided to adopt the list, suitably changed to meet its own clinical and economic needs, would depend in large part on which types of purchases would be involved. The effect would probably be modest if the formulary approach were applied only to drugs purchased for use in government hospitals, clinics, dispensaries, and similar facilities operated for the benefit of beneficiaries of a government health insurance system. The effect would be far more substantial if the list were also applied to drugs purchased and dispensed by private physicians, private pharmacists, and private hospitals; such an approach could come close to controlling nearly all drugs permitted on the market.

"Realistically, though," says a Zambian health official, "we would expect that most countries would budget perhaps 80 or 90 percent of their drug funds for the essential drugs and earmark the other 10 or 20 percent for all others which might be needed in special circumstances."

In Mozambique, where a modified WHO list was put into effect in 1978, experts generally selected not merely the most effective and least expensive drug for each important disease, but also two or three alternatives.

Professor Antonio Ruas, head of the Therapeutics Committee in Mozambique, explained, "In 90 percent of cases of pneumonia, penicillin is OK. But you must have other drugs available for the other 10 percent."[23]

In a variety of forms, formularies are now being developed or have been put into effect in such countries as Peru, Togo, some of the Andean Pact nations (including Colombia, Ecuador, and Venezuela),[24] and in Guatemala, Panama, and Bolivia.[25]

A particularly fascinating formulary has been developed with the blessings of the Ministry of Health in Kenya by a group known as AMREF (for the African Medical Research Foundation) or more popularly as the Flying Doctors. Started by two British physicians about the time of the Mau Mau troubles in the early 1960s, it operates now in Kenya, Tanzania, the Sudan, once again in Uganda, and occasionally in Malawi and Somalia. It fills three main functions: a flying ambulance service to bring patients from the back country to hospitals, a radio network service to offer consultation to physicians and paramedics in outlying areas, and a program that flies medical experts to remote districts to give intensive training programs to physicians, nurses, and physician aides.

In 1980, AMREF published a small pamphlet by a group of drug experts which not merely recommends the drugs of first, second, and sometimes third choice for each major illness but also indicates the typical cost per day for each drug treatment.[26] "It will probably be in for some strong criticism from the drug industry," says Christopher Wood, the London- and Harvard-trained physician who now directs the Flying Doctors. "But we think it will let the countries accomplish more good with the money they have to spend."[27]

It may be worthy of note to mention that, in every country in Africa and Asia in which we worked, virtually every major drug company was still officially opposed to the formulary concept. But, without exception, every drug company representative with whom we talked told us unofficially that the coming of the formularies is inevitable. Said a representative of an American firm:

> You can't stop the trend. The poor countries want it. They need it. Unquestionably, it will harm some firms. A few that do no research or development on their own and market only products that are merely expensive junk may be forced out of business. As for the rest of us? Well, a formulary may induce us to change some of our marketing strategies. But we can live with it.

They can live with it, they insist, if it covers only government purchase. If it covers both government and private purchase, this could be a disaster.

GROUP PURCHASE

There is ample precedent for attempting to purchase in large quantities in order to qualify for maximum discounts and to buy on the world market on the basis of competitive bids. Although this technique is customary in the case of many commodities, it has not been so widely applied—especially in the Third World—where drugs are concerned. Competitive bidding would, in many instances, open the way for generic companies—usually offering their products at lower prices—to win contracts. Such a prospect is usually not pleasing to most brand-name companies, which have frequently charged that generics are of low quality and cannot be trusted.

Group purchasing can be applied within a single nation, as when a single purchasing agency can request bids for drugs to be dispensed by all physicians, pharmacies, and hospitals, public or private, in the country. Greater savings can probably be achieved when several countries buy through a single agency.

Several of these multinational operations have already been used. UNICEF, which has long been in the international drug-procurement business, has let its own system be used for buying some drugs for the benefit of Third World countries. UNICEF prices for drugs bought in bulk are reportedly often as low as one-half of those in the marketplace, and sometimes as low as one-fourth.[28] But UNICEF officials have indicated that they have no intention of becoming the drug-purchasing agency for the whole Third World. This, they feel, is not their proper function. They are willing to provide temporary aid for countries that intend to set up their own drug-purchasing systems.[29]

A second program involves the Joint Mission Hospitals Equipment Board (ECHO), working in cooperation with the Netherlands-based International Dispensary Association (IDA), which is purchasing drugs for roughly a thousand mission and charity hospitals in about eighty developing countries. ECHO and IDA have also been able to assist these developing countries in buying on the world market. "Manufacturers come running to us because of our large orders," officials say. Their prices are said to be approximately 30 to 40 percent less than those which individual countries could get on their own.[30]

Other group-purchasing programs are now being started in twelve countries with a population of about 15 million in what is known as the Caribbean Community, and are being planned in a group of nations in the western Pacific. Still others will most probably be developed.

Predictably, especially since low-cost generic products are involved, the group-purchase programs have been opposed by the multinational brand-name companies and their supporters in medicine and pharmacy.[31] Also predictably, the brand-name companies warn that if their profits are reduced, they will be forced to reduce their research.

QUALITY CONTROL

Vital to the success of any drug-procurement program, and certainly to its acceptability, is an effective system of quality control: it must assure that defective products are never released for use. Reliable manufacturers have such a system. Other firms evidently do not.

It is said in drug-making that if anything can go wrong, sooner or later it will. In the past, there have been drugs bottled with the wrong label. Some have the wrong strength. With some, the active ingredient is released too rapidly, too slowly, incompletely, or not at all, and the levels reached in the blood are too high or too low. Some products have disintegrated after brief storage. Some have exploded. Some have been contaminated with penicillin or other agents to which many patients are allergic, or with powdered glass, metal particles, hair, rodent droppings, parts of insects, or living bacteria. Some have been adulterated, with the drug being replaced by useless flour or chalk.

The production of such disastrous medicines has not happened often, but it has happened.[32] A defective product may be without any effect, and a controllable disease will remain uncontrolled, or the drug itself may cause injury. It may cause death.

A country (or a hospital, a pharmacist, or a physician), in deciding whether or not to approve or purchase a particular product, may elect to accept the assurance of the manufacturer that the quality is high. This has generally proved to be safe, but there have been unhappy and even tragic exceptions. As another approach, the potential buyer may choose to accept only those products which have been approved for use in the United States, Great Britain, and other countries which maintain a highly effective control system. As still another alternative, a country could establish its own testing program.

In comparison with other phases of drug production, quality control is not fearsomely expensive. Nevertheless, special laboratory facilities are required, there is need for a high degree of technical and scientific skill, and with some drugs it may be necessary to include tests on human subjects to measure rates of absorption and blood levels. Accordingly, especially in the Third World, it may be preferable to have several countries pool their resources and create a joint program.

It may be desirable, at least at the outset, to apply rigid testing to only those drugs which have life-and-death importance, those which have a record of being involved frequently in quality problems, and those from manufacturers whose own quality-control systems are questionable. It must be emphasized that the products should be tested, whether they are made at home or abroad.

A proposal has been made that the whole matter of quality control should be turned over to an organization like WHO, which would operate an international quality-control program. This would appear to be completely impractical at present. WHO, however, should establish quality-control standards for worldwide guidance.

Finally, it should be noted that if a defective drug product is detected in one country, there is still no simple way to bring this information quickly to the attention of every other country. The situation must be corrected.

TWO-TIER PRICING

The drug industry has often been urged to set up a two-tier pricing system: one set of prices for industrialized nations and a lower set for developing countries. What seems to be the first major company to implement such a policy is Ciba-Geigy in Switzerland, with its Servipharm program established in 1978. By 1980, the new subsidiary was reaching about 40 million patients in forty-five Third World countries.

So far, Servipharm is marketing about thirty different products, nearly all of them included in the WHO list of essential drugs. Although the company has not endorsed the formulary concept, it has stated that Ciba-Geigy's profit motives and the essential-drugs list are "not mutually exclusive."

The Servipharm products can be properly considered to be branded generics. Each is backed by Ciba-Geigy's highly respected quality-control program. Prices of the Servipharm line are set at or below the cost of the least expensive generic products of acceptable quality available on the world market.

In addition to providing pharmaceuticals, the Servipharm program incorporates the training of personnel and the provision of educational materials in the developing countries. Plans for the future include the establishment of local quality control programs in some Third World nations.[33]

Other companies have proposed different approaches. For example, a group of European multinational companies has made an offer to WHO to supply essential drugs at reduced prices for the rural populations in the least developed of the developing countries, but no program has yet been put into effect; it is not clear whether the delay has been caused by unacceptable strings attached to the offer, by foot-dragging in WHO, or by a lack of interest within the Third World.

LABELING AND PROMOTION

To demand that the labeling and promotion of a drug should be precisely the same in every country would be nonsensical. The actions of a particular product may be influenced by the nutritional status and the diet of the patient, perhaps by genetic factors that may be significant in one population but unimportant in another, by different climates and different storage conditions, and by the ability of the patient to read and follow instructions. But the actions of a drug company in exaggerating the usefulness of its products or failing to disclose hazards are unpardonable.

Inaccurate drug promotion had often been charged in the past, but usually without much supporting evidence. In 1976, we were able to produce that evidence from a study conducted in depth in a number of Latin American countries and involving American, Swiss, French, and West German multinational companies. It was painfully clear that, with only a few exceptions, the labeling and promotion of the products studied were incomplete, inaccurate, and marked by exaggerated claims and the failure to disclose hazards. When the companies asserted that they were not violating any laws of the South and Central American countries, it was obvious that, at least in some instances, they were lying.

Moreover, as a result of faulty information given to physicians and pharmacists, Latin American patients were being injured or even killed. What were supposedly prescriptions for health had become prescriptions for death.

Our findings were published in May of 1976 and, in that same month, presented at a two-day committee hearing in the U.S. Senate.[34] The immediate results were not what we had anticipated. Within two days, our report was carried on the wires of United Press International, the Associated Press, Reuters, and other news services. It was reported in newspapers and on radio and television throughout Latin America and the United States, and also in Canada and Europe. Latin American embassies in Washington, D.C., telephoned us or even sent representatives to request further data.

The reaction of the industry was also somewhat unexpected. At one emergency meeting of industry leaders several urged that some steps be taken to disprove our report. One official, however, reportedly said,

"Look, I've been telling you fellows for more than ten years to cut it out or you'd be caught. Well, they've caught you. You can't disprove a damn thing."

The American industry took a significant step when the Pharmaceutical Manufacturers Association quickly passed a resolution that called for important changes. The resolution was next taken to a meeting of the directors of the International Federation of Pharmaceutical Manufacturers Associations. It was passed by the IFPMA by unanimous vote. It read as follows:

International Labeling of Prescription Medicines

WHEREAS, The world pharmaceutical industry accepts a responsibility to provide guidance concerning prescription drug product labeling for its constituent organizations, appropriate health regulatory agencies and the medical and allied professions; and

WHEREAS, The pharmaceutical industry recognizes the importance of individual national control over the labeling of prescription products to conform to the legal, regulatory and medical practices of each nation; and

WHEREAS, The International Federation of Pharmaceutical Manufacturers Associations wishes to contribute affirmatively to efforts to ensure appropriate pharmaceutical labeling consistent with individual national policies; be it therefore

Resolved, That

1. Prescription products labeling directed to health practitioners by manufacturers of prescription products, directly or through sponsored insertions in prescribing guides, should be consistent with the body of scientific and medical evidence pertaining to that product, taking into account good medical practice and the requirements of each government's regulatory authorities.

2. Particular care should be taken that essential information as to medical products' safety, contraindications and side effects is appropriately communicated.

And be it further resolved that the Secretariat of the IFPMA distribute the foregoing resolution to all member associations, with the request that each association encourage compliance among its member companies with this proposal.

The resolution had no force of law. It was simply a recommendation to drug companies all over the world. But it seems to have had an effect.

Two years later, in the fall of 1978, we returned to Latin America. We were welcomed by an old friend, Emilio Rosenstein, the publisher of the *Diccionarios de Especialidades Farmacéuticas.* "Blast you!" he said. "The companies have made so many changes in the promotional material they sent me that my new edition is many months late in going to press." We discovered that more than half of the companies concerned had radically altered their promotion. They were limiting their claims to those which could be supported with substantial scientific evidence, and they were disclosing the most important hazards. They were saying essentially the same things to physicians in Latin America that they were telling physicians in the United States.

We do not fully understand the reasons for such a change. Undoubtedly, the PMA and IFPMA resolutions had some influence. In some companies, top officials told us they had been unaware of what their foreign subsidiaries had been doing and ordered them to mend their ways. Some firms were almost certainly influenced by editorial criticism in both the United States and the Latin American press, and by Latin American health officials. In some instances, the companies acted after meetings in which angry stockholders denounced company officials and called for an end to deceitful, inaccurate promotion.

Although the promotional performance of many multinationals had been disgraceful, we were impressed by the labeling and promotion of a few firms, notably Merck, Eli Lilly, and Syntex. These companies, and others, including Smith Kline & French, no longer permit their subsidiaries or representatives in foreign countries to decide on their own how their products are to be labeled. Such decisions are made only at corporate headquarters, a policy which means that their labeling throughout the world generally follows FDA guidelines. This approach has apparently not caused undue financial suffering.

"At Syntex," says board chairman Albert Bowers, "we have always believed that you can tell the truth and still make a decent, reasonable profit."[35] In Mexico City, his predecessor, George Rosenkrantz, told us several years ago, "The explanation is really very simple. When we tell the truth, we sleep better at night."

Unfortunately, the clean-up process in Latin America is not nearing completion, and it has barely begun in Africa and Asia.

In the summer of 1981, IFPMA took what its leaders heralded as a momentous step. It issued a code of performance (see the Appendix) which called upon all its members to conduct all their dealings with government agencies, health professionals, and the public with "complete candor." Drug companies should limit their claims to what could be supported by scientific fact and should disclose important risks. Entertainment at drug company seminars or other meetings should be restrained and conducted with dignity in keeping with the scientific nature of the occasion. Free samples to physicians should be limited—but the door was left open to give a physician whatever he requested. There were, however, no provisions for monitoring the code or enforcing it.

IFPMA officials were enthusiastic about the new code, declaring that the multinational drug industry was now accepting its social responsibilities. They also suggested that there was no longer any need for tighter drug regulation. But the code was described as "vague, incomplete, amateurish rubbish, done just to clean up their image, designed to impress and not to work."[36] Even within the industry, there were some who scoffed at the code. An official of one American firm said, "It carries all the threat of the Boy Scout oath."

The greatest weakness in the IFPMA code was the lack of even a hint of some kind of machinery to make it work. Critics were reassured that compliance could be safely left to voluntary action by individual companies, but most critics remained unreassured. Any suggestion that implementation might be developed through an arrangement with WHO or any other international agency met with what appeared to be universal opposition from the industry. Especially if the labeling program were to be combined with a program to evaluate drug product efficacy and quality, representatives of the drug companies declared that the results would inevitably include more regulatory restrictions and a slowdown in the development of new drugs. Further, if experts from "centrally-planned economy countries"—that is to say, socialist nations—were to participate in the review processes, confidential trade secrets might be leaked.

In October 1981, the idea that the industry was unanimously against any such plan was demolished. Walter von Wartburg, a spokesman for Ciba-Geigy in Basel, told an American television team:

> I would propose that if any one body—be it the FDA, your Food and Drug Administration organization, be it the World Health Organization, be it any respected big organization—takes over the whole task of standardizing by saying this is drug X, it can have the following indications,

it must have the following contraindications, and we would be more than happy to comply with that on a worldwide basis . . . it would reduce our costs, it would reduce the burden of dealing with hundreds of authorities at the same time, and it would reduce the burden of the medical people who sometimes get different kinds of information through the different sources.[37]

Most other multinational drug companies were astonished by van Wartburg's statement, and some were quick to express their displeasure. Ciba-Geigy, they emphasized, is only one company. Von Wartburg freely admitted that his plan would not be easy to put into effect. Ciba-Geigy is, however, one of the most influential multinationals in the world. Efforts might be made to ignore its ideas, but those candid views will not be quickly forgotten.

In the matter of drug promotion and labeling, consumers, particularly in the Third World, have neglected to utilize one procedure that has long been available. In its charter, which was approved by all its member nations, WHO is allowed to intervene to standardize the information supplied with a number of types of products moving in international commerce, including pharmaceuticals. In any country, consumers might well pressure their government to insist on WHO intervention when any drug company promotion may pose a threat to health or life. So far as we can determine, no developing country has ever demanded enforcement of this provision.

A TASK FOR CONSUMERS

Intimately involved in the whole matter of drug discovery, production, pricing, promotion, prescribing, dispensing, and use are the people who are the patients, the taxpayers, and sometimes the stockholders. The activities of drug companies can affect their dividends, their taxes, and their lives. Especially during the past five years, consumers have taken a growing interest in almost every facet of medication. This, as consumers have learned, is a highly complicated field, touching on such areas as modern pharmacology, high technology, corporate financing, international transfer pricing, patient-physician relations, capitalist-socialist rivalries, and what are or should be the goals of drug research. A number of questions remain unanswered: Are the industrialized nations obligated to pay, perhaps as a kind of indemnity, for the drug needs of developing countries? Which should be given top priority, filling the drug needs of the Third World or developing better drugs for future generations? How long should bribery and corruption be condoned when these age-old practices may result in injury or death?

During the last few years, a number of consumer groups have shown increasing interest in the marketing of drugs and the policies of drug companies. Among the most important are the International Organization of Consumers Unions (IOCU), based in The Hague; two British groups, Social Audit in London and OXFAM in Oxford; and a newly formed organization, Health Action International (HAI), which was established in Geneva in the summer of 1981.

Under the direction of its president, Anwar Fazal of Malaysia, who was reelected in 1981 to serve a second three-year term, IOCU has long been interested in product safety and consumer protection. It is now setting up an international information network to collect and disseminate vital material on drugs to the public, to physicians and other health professionals, and to governmental health agencies, especially in the Third World. It is already distributing information on several dozen different drug products that have been barred from some markets or put under severe restrictions—with at least a suggestion that other countries might do well to take similar steps. It may collect information on serious adverse drug reactions reported in any country and see that all countries are warned. It intends to seek out qualified manufacturers that might be induced to produce and market low-cost products under generic name to the Third World. It is urging developing countries to set up group purchasing and quality-control programs.

In the same way, Social Audit and OXFAM have been studying drug promotion, drug pricing, bribery, and the prescribing practices of physicians. Social Audit has already publicized the dangers of such products as Lomotil and clioquinol.

Perhaps the most militant of these organizations is HAI (which happens to be the German word for "shark"). It was created to "resist the ill-treatment of consumers by multinational drug companies." Anwar Fazal, head of the IOCU, said:

> We have different priorities, but we agree on the diagnosis. We agree unanimously that the multinational drug industry is deeply implicated in the trade of hazardous, useless, inappropriate, and often unconscionably expensive drugs. And we are unanimously agreed that we will not toler-

ate this ill-treatment of consumers—particularly when they are sick and poor.

The primary target of HAI appears to be all multinational drug companies, even though some may be striving to do a decent job. "It is not appropriate for us to give, so to speak, a balanced view," Charles Medawar of Social Audit told a IOCU meeting in the Netherlands. "The multinationals can be counted on to say all the nice things about multinationals." Medawar spoke for many activists when he added, "The British companies abroad represent the new diplomacy. If Glaxo or Beecham screws up in somebody else's country, I feel strongly responsible. I do not wish to be represented in that way. I feel an obligation to protest vigorously."[38]

HAI is calling for an end to brand names and the promotional methods used to sell them. It is urging national governments to stop the dumping of dangerous or useless drug products by their companies. It is calling for lower prices on all drug products and certainly on essential products for Third World buyers. A ceiling should be placed on drug company profits, it is claimed, and there should be an end to drug patents—especially on essential drugs—because the products are vital for health. (See Drug Patents, above.)

Some consumer activists are suggesting the possibility of even more drastic steps: nationalizing the drug companies or turning them into public utilities, taking action in the courts and filing damage suits against manufacturers for drug-induced injury to patients, and mounting international boycotts. They are working with WHO experts to produce a WHO pharmaceutical marketing code which, unlike the IFPMA's code, would provide for monitoring, enforcement, and sanctions against offenders.

Although no WHO drug code has yet been introduced, the multinational companies have already reacted or overreacted. They fear they will be saddled by still more regulations in the Third World, and perhaps in some industrialized nations as well, even though the record of developing countries in enforcing their existing laws and regulations has not been particularly impressive. But if a code were to call for such things as high product quality, honest labeling, and reasonable prices, it would merely require the companies to do what they say they are already doing. If it were to call for some kind of national formulary, many multinational firms have already indicated that they could live with such an approach. Further, such a code would offer only recommendations and guidelines. The provisions would probably not have the force of law unless and until they were supported by international treaties.

If, however, a WHO code included what were deemed to be intolerable demands, this might prove to be the last straw. The United States, perhaps joined by Great Britain and West Germany, already unhappy and frustrated by the manner in which they have increasingly been blocked, dominated, and bitterly denounced in a number of areas by coalitions of small countries—and, at the same time, berated for their unwillingness to provide more and more funding—might possibly take the step they have been seriously considering, and simply withdraw from WHO. Such a move would be difficult, requiring action at the highest levels of government. At this time, we would not endorse it. But it would not be impossible.

Regardless of all the impassioned charges and countercharges and the other purple rhetoric that may be involved, these points seem to be clear:

— Patients cannot be heavily blamed for their intense desire to have a pill for every ill. The will to survive is strong.

— While some physicians in the Third World practice superb medicine, others do not. Some have neglected to do their homework, to keep up-to-date on scientific knowledge, to resist corruption. In each Third World country, some physicians and various drug experts—probably more dedicated and certainly more courageous than their colleagues—have risked professional censure and personal attacks in seeking to remove needless or dangerous products from the marketplace. They have fought to prevent the approval of unneeded new ones, to improve the prescribing patterns of physicians, to induce government and private purchasing agencies to allocate their available drug funds more wisely, to expose bribery, and to demand honesty and accuracy in drug labeling. Most physicians and most medical organizations have so far accomplished little or nothing in these fields.

— In the United States, Great Britain, and other countries, substantial

control of dishonest or inaccurate drug labeling, irrational prescribing, the promotion of unsafe or ineffective products, and prof-
it-motivated attacks against low-cost products was eventually
achieved by government actions. These actions, however, became
possible only after the public had been informed by the press, radio, and television. The media in developing countries may need to
take similar steps. Where newspapers, magazines, and radio and
television stations are government-controlled or government-
owned or subject to intense pressures from business or industry,
taking any such steps may call for a high degree of courage. A few
reporters and their editors in the Third World—for example, in
Colombia, Brazil, Mexico, Kenya, and Tanzania—have already
displayed such bravery. Others must follow in their footsteps.

— Many drug companies, multinational and domestic, have brought
upon their heads much deserved criticism. Sanctimoniously, they
have proclaimed their virtues and denied their failings. They remind one of the early missionaries who reputedly went to Hawaii
to do good and who did exceedingly well. The appropriate objective for these companies would seem to be obvious: instead of de-
voting so much effort, mainly through costly public relations campaigns, to clean up the industry's public image, the companies
may find it more profitable in the long run to clean up the industry.

Finally, it is our belief that, within the international drug industry in
general and the American industry in particular, change is possible. It
may even now be taking place. There seems to be a new generation of
industry leaders who are willing to move in the direction of decency,
dignity, and social responsibility. We wish them well, and remind them
that the price may not be too great.

As we noted above, one company leader says, "You can tell the truth
and still make a decent, reasonable profit."

APPENDIX

IFPMA CODE OF PHARMACEUTICAL MARKETING PRACTICES

(International Federation of Pharmaceutical Manufacturers Associations)

PREAMBLE

The Statute of the Federation article 3 states that one of the objects of the Federation is "to promote and support continuous development throughout the pharmaceutical industry of ethical principles and practices voluntarily agreed on" and "to coordinate the efforts of its members towards the realization of the above objects".

It is believed that in keeping with the pharmaceutical industry's international responsibilities, the members of the Federation will be prepared to accept certain obligations, insofar as their marketing practices are concerned, and to ensure respect for them.

IFPMA recommends a Code of Marketing Practices to its member associations, recognizing the difficulty of setting out a simple Code which will be applicable in all parts of the world. It seems clear that national and regional conditions and legal restrictions will continue to vary to such an extent as to make a simple world Code impractical. Nevertheless, the Federation believes that it has a duty to encourage its member associations to either introduce such Codes of Practices or where such Codes already exist, to continually re-examine and where necessary revise them so that a voluntary system based on such a Code keeps pace with modern medical knowledge and changing health services and conditions.

It is recognized that many individual member associations of IFPMA have laid down their own Codes of Marketing Practices and this recommended Code is not intended to replace similar Codes or instruments already in force by members of the Federation. The following voluntary Code is therefore put forward as a model for IFPMA's member associations.

A Code of Marketing Practices of this sort should be the responsibility of member associations who should also provide guidance to their members on matters of compliance and interpretation.

OBLIGATIONS OF INDUSTRY

The obligations of the industry may be identified as follows:
The pharmaceutical industry, conscious of its special position arising from its involvement in public health, and justifiably eager to fulfill its obligations in a free and fully responsible manner, undertakes:

— to ensure that all products it makes available for prescription purposes to the public are backed by the fullest technological service and have full regard to the needs of public health;

— to produce pharmaceutical products under adequate procedures and strict quality assurance;

— to base the claims for substances and formulations on valid scientific evidence, thus determining the therapeutic indications and conditions of use;

— to provide scientific information with objectivity and good taste, with scrupulous regard for truth, and with clear statements with respect to indications, contraindications, tolerance and toxicity;

— to use complete candour in dealings with public health officials, health care professionals and the public.

SUGGESTED CODE OF MARKETING PRACTICES

We hereby declare our intention to voluntarily conform to the following Code of Marketing Practices:

I. General Principles

1. The term "pharmaceutical product" in this concept means any pharmaceutical or biological product intended for use in the diagnosis, cure, mitigation, treatment or prevention of disease in humans, or to affect the structure or any function of the human body, which is promoted and advertised to the medical profession rather than directly to the lay public.

2. Information on pharmaceutical products should be accurate, fair and objective, and presented in such a way as to conform not only to legal requirements but also to ethical standards and to standards of good taste.

3. Information should be based on an up to date evaluation of all the available scientific evidence, and should reflect this evidence clearly.

4. No public communication shall be made with the intent of promoting a pharmaceutical product as safe and effective for any use before the required approval of the pharmaceutical product for marketing for such use is obtained. However, this provision is not intended to abridge the right of the scientific community and the public to be fully informed concerning scientific and medical progress. It is not intended to restrict a full and proper exchange of scientific information concerning a pharmaceutical product, including appropriate dissemination of investigational findings in scientific or lay communications media, nor to restrict public disclosure to stockholders and others concerning any pharmaceutical product as may be required or desirable under law, rule or regulation.

5. Statements in promotional communications should be based upon substantial scientific evidence or other responsible medical opinion. Claims should not be stronger than such evidence warrants. Every effort should be made to avoid ambiguity.

6. Particular care should be taken that essential information as to pharmaceutical products' safety, contraindications and side effects or toxic hazards is appropriately and consistently communicated subject to the legal, regulatory and medical practices of each nation. The word "safe" must not be used without qualification.

7. Promotional communications should have medical clearance, or where appropriate, clearance by the responsible pharmacist, before their release.

II. Medical Representatives

Medical representatives must be adequately trained and possess sufficient medical and technical knowledge to present information on their company's products in an accurate and responsible manner.

III. Symposia, Congresses and other Means of Verbal Communication

Symposia, congresses and the like are indispensable for the dissemination of knowledge and experience. Scientific objectives should be the principal focus in arranging such meetings, and entertainment and other hospitality shall not be inconsistent with such objectives.

IV. Printed Promotional Material

Scientific and technical information shall fully disclose the properties of the pharmaceutical product as approved in the country in question based on current scientific knowledge including:

— The active ingredients, using the approved names where such names exist.

— At least one approved indication for use together with the dosage and method of use.

— A succinct statement of the side-effects, precautions and contraindications.

Except for pharmaceutical products where use entails specific precautionary measures, reminders need not necessarily contain all the above information providing that a form of words is used which indicates clearly that further information is available on request.

Promotional material, such as mailings and medical journal advertisements, must not be designed to disguise their real nature and the frequency and volume of such mailings should not be offensive to the health care professionals.

V. Samples

Samples may be supplied to the medical and allied professions to familiarize them with the products, to enable them to gain experience with the product in their practice, or upon request.

REFERENCES

In the following pages, certain frequently cited references are abbreviated as follows:

Goodman and Gilman = Louis S. Goodman and Alfred Gilman (eds.), *The Pharmacological Basis of Therapeutics* (New York: Macmillan, 4th ed., 1970, and 6th ed., 1980).

Martindale = Ainley Wade (ed.), *Martindale: The Extra Pharmacopoeia* (London: Pharmaceutical Press, 27th ed., 1977).

AMA Drug Evaluations = American Medical Association, Department of Drugs, *AMA Drug Evaluations* (Chicago: American Medical Association, 4th ed., 1980).

Pills, Profits, and Politics = Milton Silverman and Philip R. Lee, *Pills, Profits, and Politics* (Berkeley: University of California Press, 1974).

Drugging of the Americas = Milton Silverman, *The Drugging of the Americas* (Berkeley: University of California Press, 1976).

1. THE PATIENTS

1. Dianna Melrose, *The Great Health Robbery: Baby Milk and Medicines in Yemen* (Oxford: OXFAM, 1981).

2. John Yudkin (Whittington Hospital, London), personal communications, 1980, 1981.

3. Dianna Melrose, *Great Health Robbery*.

4. John Fry and W. A. J. Farndale (eds.), *International Medical Care* (Oxford and Lancaster, England: Medical and Technical Publishing, 1972); Richard A. Smith (ed.), *Manpower and Primary Health Care: Guidelines for Improving/Expanding Health Services Coverage in Developing Countries* (Honolulu: University of Hawaii Press, 1978); Philip R. Lee and Patricia E. Franks, "Health and Disease in the Community," *Mobius* 1:5 (April 1981).

5. James Kagia (Faculty of Medicine, University of Nairobi, Kenya), personal communication, 1980.

6. Colin Forbes (Kenyatta National Hospital, Nairobi, Kenya), personal communication, 1980.

7. P. F. D'Arcy (Queen's University, Belfast, Ireland), personal communication, 1980.

8. Colin Forbes, personal communication, 1980.

9. John Yudkin, personal communication, 1980.

10. John Yudkin, personal communication, 1980; Dianna Melrose, *Great Health Robbery*.

11. John Yudkin.

12. Halfdan Mahler, recorded in "In Sickness or in Wealth," British Broadcasting Corporation, Radio Four, September 2, 1979.

13. Patience Vince, idem.

14. N. D. Wilfred Lionel (University of Colombo, Sri Lanka), personal communication, 1980.

15. Ingemar Gahnstedt (Ministry of Health, Kenya), personal communication, 1980.

16. Christopher Wood (African Medical and Research Foundation, Nairobi, Kenya), personal communication, 1980.

17. William L. Minkowski, "An American Physician in Rural West Africa," *Western Journal of Medicine* 134:267 (March 1981).

18. Foo Gaik Sim (International Organization of Consumers Unions, Penang, Malaysia), personal communication, 1980; Matthew Gwee (University of Singapore), personal communication, 1980; N. D. Wilfred Lionel, personal communication, 1980.

19. Patience Vince, recorded in "In Sickness or in Wealth"; Dianna Melrose, *Great Health Robbery*.

20. John Yudkin, recorded in "In Sickness or in Wealth," BBC (Radio), Sept. 2, 1979; N. D. Wilfred Lionel, personal communication, 1980; V. T. Herat Gunaratne, "Bringing down Drug Costs: The Sri Lankan Example," *World Health Forum:* 1:117 (1980); John Yudkin, cited in "Drugs and Their Markets," *Guardian* (London), August 16, 1977; Ministry of Health, Zambia, personal communication, 1980.

21. Health Care Financing Administration, personal communication, 1981; Herat Gunaratne, "Bringing down Drug Costs."

22. John Yudkin, personal communication, 1980, 1981.

23. G. Upunda, J. Yudkin, and G. Brown, *Therapeutic Guidelines. A Manual to Assist in the Rational Purchase and Prescription of Drugs* (Nairobi, Kenya: African Medical and Research Foundation, 1980).

24. Colin Forbes, personal communication, 1980.

25. John Yudkin, personal communication.

26. Nairobi, Kenya, *Weekly Review*, October 24, 1980.

27. John Yudkin.

2. THE DRUGS

1. *Pills, Profits, and Politics,* chapters 3, 12; *Drugging of the Americas,* chapters 1, 9.

2. Robert J. Ledogar, *Hungry for Profits* (New York: IDOC/North America, 1975).

3. *Drugging of the Americas.*

4. Wolfgang Howorka, "Dangerous Drugs," in *Consumer Action in Developing Countries* (Penang, Malaysia: International Organization of Consumers Unions, 1980).

5. Sanjaya Lall, "The International Pharmaceutical Industry and Less Developed Countries," *Oxford Bulletin of Economics and Statistics* 36:143–172 (August 1974).

6. John S. Yudkin, "Provision of Medicines in a Developing Country," *Lancet* 1:810 (April 15, 1978).

7. Charles Medawar, *Insult or Injury* (London: Social Audit, 1979); Charles Medawar, *Drug Disinformation* (London: Social Audit, 1980).

8. Haslemere Group, *Who Needs the Drug Companies?* (London: Haslemere, 1976).

9. T. Heller, *Poor Health, Rich Profits* (Nottingham: Spokesman Books, 1977).

10. *Physicians' Desk Reference* (Oradell, N.J.: Medical Economics, 1980).

11. Colin Duncan (ed.), *MIMS* (London: Haymarket Publishing, 1980).

12. *MIMS Africa* (London: Morgan Publications, 1980).

13. Ng Chu Teck (ed.), *IIMS* (Hong Kong: IMS Pacific, 1980).

14. Ng Chu Teck (ed.), *DIMS* (Hong Kong; IMS Pacific, 1980).

15. Ng Chu Teck (ed.), *PIMS* (Hong Kong: IMS Pacific, 1980).

16. Emilio Rosenstein (ed.), *Diccionario de Especialidades Farmacéuticas, Edición C.A.D.* (Mexico City: Impresora y Editora Mexicana, 11th ed., 1979).

17. *Pills, Profits, and Politics,* p. 75.

18. Medawar, *Drug Disinformation,* p. 3.14.

19. *Drugging of the Americas.*

20. Louis S. Goodman and Alfred Gilman (eds.), *The Pharmacological Basis of Therapeutics* (New York: Macmillan, 4th ed., 1970, and 6th ed., 1980).

21. American Medical Association, Department of Drugs, *AMA Drug Evaluations* (Chicago: American Medical Association, 4th ed., 1980).

22. Ainley Wade (ed.), *Martindale: The Extra Pharmacopoeia* (London: Pharmaceutical Press, 27th ed., 1977).

23. Iwan Darmansjah (University of Indonesia), personal communication, 1980.

24. William R. McCabe, Bernard E. Kreger, and Margaret Johns, "Type-Specific and Cross-Reactive Antibodies in Gram-Negative Bacteremia," *New England Journal of Medicine* 287:261 (August 10, 1972); Philip R. Lee, statement in U.S. Senate, Select Committee on Small Business, Subcommittee on Monopoly, *Present Status of Competition in the Pharmaceutical Industry* 32: 15377, 15425-15427 (1976).

25. *Martindale,* p. 1108; *AMA Drug Evaluations,* pp. 1249-1251; Goodman and Gilman, 1980, pp. 1195, 1196.

26. Goodman and Gilman, 1970, p. 1273.

27. Russel Chen, personal communication, Taipei, Taiwan, 1980.

28. *AMA Drug Evaluations,* pp. 1265-1270; Goodman and Gilman, 1980, p. 1187; *Martindale,* pp. 1186-1188.

29. *Martindale,* pp. 1146, 1147; *AMA Drug Evaluations,* pp. 1261-1263; Goodman and Gilman, 1970, pp. 1296, 1297.

30. *AMA Drug Evaluations,* p. 1261.

31. Iwan Darmansjah, personal communication, Jakarta, 1980.

32. *Pills, Profits, and Politics,* pp. 125-134.

33. Louis Weinstein, "Chemotherapy of Microbial Disease," in Goodman and Gilman, 1970, p. 1159.

34. *AMA Drug Evaluations,* p. 1276.

35. Norman A. David, N. M. Phatak, and F. B. Zener, "Iodochlorhydroxyquinoline and Diiodohydroxyquinoline: Animal Toxicity and Absorption in Man," *American Journal of Tropical Diseases* 24:29 (1944).

36. Norman A. David, "Uncontrolled Use of Oral Amebecides," *Journal of the American Medical Association* 129:572 (October 20, 1945).

37. Hamilton Anderson, personal communications, 1980, 1981.

38. B. H. Kean and Somerset R. Waters, "The Diarrhea of Travelers. III. Drug Prophylaxis in Mexico," *New England Journal of Medicine* 261:71 (July 9, 1959).

39. Cited in Olle Hansson, "Oxyquinoline Intoxication Outside Japan, Its Recognition and the Scope of the Problem," in T. Soda (ed.), *Drug-Induced Sufferings: Medical, Pharmaceutical and Legal Aspects* (Amsterdam: Excerpta Medica, 1980), p. 429.

40. Ibid., p. 430.

41. Lennart Berggren and Olle Hansson, "Absorption of Intestinal Antiseptics Derived from 8-Hydroxyquinolines," *Journal of Clinical Pharmacology and Therapeutics* 9:67 (1968).

42. Zenzo Tamura, cited in Tadao Tsubaki, "Etiology of SMON. An Early Study and Its Development," in *Drug-Induced Sufferings,* p. 423.

43. Oliver Gillie, "How Safe Is This Holiday-Tummy Pill?" *Sunday Times* (London), May 22, 1977.

44. Tadeo Tsubaki, Yoshiaki Honma, and Makoto Hoshi, "Neurological Syndrome Associated with Clioquinol," *Lancet* 1:696 (April 3, 1971).

45. Toshio Higashida, "The Characteristics and Prevention of Drug-Induced Suffering in Japan," in *Drug-Induced Sufferings,* pp. 401, 402.

46. Olle Hansson, *Arzneimittel-Multis und der SMON-Skandal* (Berlin: Arzneimittel-Informations-Dienst GmbH, 1979), pp. 34, 35.

47. Ibid. p. 36.

48. Oliver Gillie, "How Safe Is This Holiday-Tummy Pill?"

49. Kiyohiko Katahira et al., in *Drug-Induced Sufferings,* p. 441.

50. Olle Hansson, *Arzneimittel-Multis,* p. 22.

51. Etsuro Totsuka, Keiji Shibuya, and Tsutomu Kigasawa, "The Status of SMON Litigation in Japan," paper presented before the 10th World Congress of the International Organization of Consumers Unions, The Hague, Netherlands, June 22, 1981.

52. "Oxyquinolines," *Lancet* 1:492 (February 28, 1981).

53. Oliver Gillie, "Drug Was Sold Despite Tests That Showed It Could Blind," *Sunday Times* (London), February 22, 1981.

54. Dorothy Kweyu (Nairobi *Sunday Nation*), personal communication, Nairobi, 1980.

55. "Apology to SMON Plaintiffs by Ciba-Geigy (Japan) Ltd.," *Proceedings, Geneva Press Conference on SMON, April 28, 1980* (Tokyo: Organizing Committee of Geneva Press Conference on SMON, 1980), Appendix IV, p. 36. (Emphasis added.)

56. Charles Fish and Hamilton H. Anderson, "Mass Suppressive Therapy with Iodochlorhydroxyquin (Enterovioform-Ciba) for Amebiasis and Shigellosis in Institutions for the Mentally Retarded," paper presented before the 10th International Congress on Tropical Medicine and Malaria, Manila, Philippine Islands, November 9–15, 1980.

57. *Martindale,* p. 72; Goodman and Gilman, 1980, p. 1064; *AMA Drug Evaluations,* p. 963.

58. *AMA Drug Evaluations,* p. 1401.

59. *Medipharm: Medical Index of Pharmaceutical Specialties in Nigeria* (Ikeja, Nigeria: Literamed Publications, January–March, 1979), p. 11.

60. *Martindale,* pp. 961, 962; *AMA Drug Evaluations,* p. 966.

61. Frederick W. Madison and Theodore L. Squier, "The Etiology of Primary Granulocytopenia (Agranulocytic Angina)," *Journal of the American Medical Association* 102:755 (March 10, 1934).

62. Leader Stirling (Ministry of Health, Tanzania), personal communication, Dar es Salaam, October 1980.

63. Dal-Hyun Chi (Ministry of Health and Social Affairs, Korea), personal communication, Seoul, December 1980.

64. P. Epstein and J. S. Yudkin, "Agranulocytosis in Mozambique due to Amidopyrine, A Drug Withdrawn in the West," *Lancet* 2:254 (August 2, 1980).

65. John Yudkin, personal communication, 1981.

66. Goodman and Gilman, 1970, pp. 334, 335.

67. *Martindale,* p. 187.

68. *Drugging of the Americas,* pp. 51, 53, 59, 60.

69. Desmond Fernando, cited in "In Sickness or in Wealth," British Broadcasting Corporation, Radio Four, September 2, 1979.

70. *AMA Drug Evaluations,* pp. 653, 654; *Physicians' Desk Reference,* p. 1245.

71. *AMA Drug Evaluations,* p. 653.

72. Ibid., p. 656.

73. David Jones (Ciba-Geigy), personal communication, 1981.

74. Goodman and Gilman, 1970, p. 562.

75. Ibid., p. 1000.

76. *Pills, Profits, and Politics,* pp. 98–103.

77. Goodman and Gilman, 1980, p. 1439; *Martindale,* p. 1381; *AMA Drug Evaluations,* pp. 690–695.

78. Goodman and Gilman, 1980, pp. 1429, 1430, 1438; *Martindale,* p. 1380; *AMA Drug Evaluations,* pp. 667–669.

79. Richard A. Edgren, "On Oral Contraceptive Safety: Cardiovascular Problems," *International Journal of Fertility,* in press.

80. Goodman and Gilman, 1980, p. 1444; *Martindale,* p. 1385; *AMA Drug Evaluations,* pp. 695–701.

81. Milton Silverman in "Pesticides and Pills: For Export Only," Public Broadcasting System television broadcast, October 7, 1981.

82. *Pills, Profits, and Politics,* pp. 261–266.

3. THE PROFESSIONALS

1. Dianna Melrose, *The Great Health Robbery: Baby Milk and Medicines in Yemen* (Oxford: OXFAM, 1981).

2. *Inventory of Health Facilities, 1978: Main Report* (Dar es Salaam, Tanzania: Ministry of Health, 1979).

3. *Drugging of the Americas,* pp. 120–122.

4. Ayodele Tella (University of Lagos, Nigeria), personal communication, 1980.

5. Colin Forbes (Kenyatta National Hospital, Nairobi, Kenya), personal communication, 1980.

6. James Kagia (Faculty of Medicine, University of Nairobi, Kenya), personal communication, 1980.

7. Ayodele Tella, personal communication, 1980.

8. Albert Henn (U.S. Agency for International Development, Dar es Salaam, Tanzania), personal communication, 1980.

9. Segun Bamgbose (University of Lagos, Nigeria), personal communication, 1980; Sang Sup Lee (National University, College of Pharmacy, Seoul, Korea), personal communication, 1980.

10. Personal communications from the following: Segun Bamgbose; Iwan Darmansjah (University of Indonesia), 1980; Silvestre Frenk (Hospital de Pediatria, Mexican Institute of Social Security), 1976; James Kagia, 1980; N. D. Wilfred Lionel (University of Colombo, Sri Lanka), 1980; Nelia Corset-Maramba (University of the Philippines), 1980; Ruben Mayórga (School of Microbiology, Guatemala City), 1976; Alfonso Trejos Willis (Hospital San Juan de Dios, San José, Costa Rica), 1978.

11. Dorothy Kweyu, in Nairobi, Kenya, *Sunday Nation,* July 20, 1980.

12. Matthew Gwee (University of Singapore), personal communication, 1980.

13. Karuga Koinange (Ministry of Health, Kenya), personal communication, 1980.

14. John Yudkin (Whittington Hospital, London), personal communication, 1981.

15. *Pills, Profits, and Politics,* chapter 5.

16. Barry Newman, "Consumer Protection is Underdeveloped in the Third World," *Wall Street Journal,* April 8, 1980.

17. P. G. Moore (Ministry of Health, Zambia), personal communication, 1980.

18. P. York, "The Shelf Life of Some Antibiotic Preparations Stored Under Tropical Conditions," *Pharmazie* 32:101 (1977).

19. Mohammed Idris (Consumers' Association of Penang), cited in Barry Newman, "Consumer Protection."

20. Ayodele Tella, personal communication.

21. Mohammed Idris.

22. Matthew Gwee.

23. N. D. Wilfred Lionel.

24. Matthew Gwee.

4. THE DRUG INDUSTRY

1. *Pills, Profits, and Politics*, pp. 178–181.

2. Richard J. Barnet and Ronald E. Müller, *Global Reach: The Power of the Multinational Corporations* (New York: Simon & Schuster, 1974).

3. *Pills, Profits, and Politics*, pp. 27–33.

4. Iwan Darmansjah (University of Indonesia), personal communication, 1980.

5. Dianna Melrose (OXFAM), press statement, April 21, 1980.

6. *Pills, Profits, and Politics*, p. 55.

7. Ibid., chapters 2–8.

8. John S. Yudkin, "Withdrawal of Clonidine," *Lancet* 1:546 (March 5, 1977).

9. M. Muttalib et al., "Comparative Study of Doxycycline and Ampicillin in Respiratory Tract Infections in Bangladesh," *Modern Medicine of Aisa* 16:43 (October 1980).

10. Dianna Melrose, *The Great Health Robbery: Baby Milk and Medicines in Yemen* (Oxford: OXFAM, 1981).

11. M. C. E. Gwee and T. S. Yeoh, "Pentazocine Hydrochloride ('Talwin'): The Truth, the Whole Truth, and Nothing but the Truth," *Singapore Family Physician* 5:5 (1979).

12. *Pills, Profits, and Politics*, pp. 166–168.

13. Ibid., p. 140.

14. Milton Silverman, Philip R. Lee, and Mia Lydecker, *Pills and the Public Purse* (Berkeley: University of California Press, 1981), p. 86.

15. Ibid., chapter 10.

16. N. D. Wilfred Lionel (University of Sri Lanka, Colombo), personal communication, 1980; Dianna Melrose, press statement.

17. Dianna Melrose, idem.

18. John Yudkin, personal communications, 1980, 1981.

19. Karuga Koinange (Ministry of Health, Kenya), personal communication, 1980.

20. P. G. Moore (Ministry of Health, Zambia), personal communication, 1980.

21. Robert Richter (Robert Richter Productions, New York), personal communication, 1980.

22. Sarah Bartlett, in film presentation, 10th World Assembly, International Organization of Consumers Unions, The Hague, Netherlands, June 1981.

23. John Yudkin, cited in Martha Honey, "Tanzania May Ban West's Drug Salesmen," *Guardian* (London), August 16, 1977.

24. Ayodele Tella (University of Lagos, Nigeria), personal communication, 1980.

25. A. O. K. Obel, "Editorial—Therapeutics: A Non-Starter," *Medicom* (Kenya) 2:85 (May–June 1980).

26. Silvestre Frenk (Hospital de Pediatria, Mexican Institute of Social Security), personal communication, 1976.

27. Leader Stirling (Ministry of Health, Tanzania), personal communication, 1980.

28. "Drugs 'Reps' Reply," Dar es Salaam, Tanzania, *Sunday News* March 25, 1979.

29. José Félix Patiño (Panamerican Federation of Associations of Medical Schools, Bogotá, Colombia), personal communication, 1981.

30. Patience Vince, recorded in "In Sickness or in Wealth," British Broadcasting Corporation, Radio Four, September 2, 1979.

31. Michael Peretz, cited in "In Sickness or in Wealth," BBC (Radio).

32. "Drug 'Reps' Reply."

33. Ayodele Tella, personal communication, 1980.

34. Sang Sup Lee (National University, Seoul, Korea), personal communication, 1980.

35. *Drugging of the Americas,* chapter 9.

36. Luis Sánchez Medal (National Institute of Cardiology, Mexico City), idem., p. 109.

37. Arthur Hoppe, San Francisco *Chronicle,* May 27, 1981. Copyright 1981, Chronicle Publishing Co., reprinted by permission of the author.

5. BRIBERY

1. Ingemar Gahnstedt (Ministry of Health, Kenya), personal communication, 1980.

2. "Healthy Business," film for television, Belbo Film Productions, London, England, 1981.

3. J. Z. Galvez-Tan, cited in Dianna Melrose, "Medicines for the Very Poor: A Prescription for Change," paper presented before the International Seminar in and for Developing Countries: A Challenge for Europe; Milan, Italy, June 22–23, 1981.

4. *Pills, Profits, and Politics,* p. 78.

5. V. T. Herat Gunaratne, "Bringing Down Drug Costs: The Sri Lankan Example," *World Health Forum* 1:117 (1980).

6. Segun Bambgose (University of Lagos, Nigeria), personal communication, 1980.

7. John S. Yudkin, "Provision of Medicines in a Developing Country,"

Lancet 1:810 (April 15, 1978); John S. Yudkin, "The Economics of Pharmaceutical Supply in Tanzania," *International Journal of Health Services* 10:455 (1980).

8. John S. Yudkin, "Economics of Pharmaceutical Supply."

9. John S. Yudkin, "Provision of Medicines."

10. Gordon Adams and Sherri Zann Rosenthal, *The Invisible Hand: Questionable Corporate Payments Overseas.* (New York: Council on Economic Priorities, 1976).

11. Dal-Hyun Chi (Ministry of Health and Social Affairs, Korea), personal communication, 1980.

12. "Commerce Chief Sees Need for 'Little Bribes,'" San Francisco *Chronicle,* March 24, 1981.

13. Norman C. Miller, "U.S. Business Overseas: Back to Bribery?" *Wall Street Journal,* April 30, 1981.

14. Arsenio Regala (Food and Drugs Administration, Philippines), personal communication, 1980.

15. Kurt Langbein, Hans-Peter Martin, Hans Weiss, and Roland Werner, *Gesunde Geschäfte: Die Praktiken der Pharma-Industrie* (Cologne, West Germany: Kiepenheuer and Witsch, 1981).

6. THE OPTIONS

1. Indira Gandhi, Address to the 34th World Health Assembly, Geneva, May 16, 1981.

2. Claudia Baskin, in *PMA Newsletter,* March 2, 1981.

3. Halfdan Mahler, cited in "In Sickness or in Wealth," British Broadcasting Corporation, Radio Four, September 2, 1979.

4. *Drugging of the Americas.*

5. George Teeling-Smith, BBC Radio, "In Sickness or in Wealth."

6. Anil Agarwal, "Drugs and the Third World" (London: Earthscan Press, briefing document no. 10, August 1978); "Major Issues in Transfer of Technology to Developing Countries: A Case Study of the Pharmaceutical Industry," United Nations Conference on Trade and Development (UNCTAD), Trade Development Board, Committee on Transfer of Technology, Geneva, November 24 1975; *Technology Policies and Planning for the Pharmaceutical Sector in the Developing Countries* (Geneva: UNCTAD, 1980).

7. U.S. Department of Health, Education, and Welfare, Office of the Secretary, Task Force on Prescription Drugs, *Final Report* (Washington, D.C.: U.S. Government Printing Office, 1969).

8. Harold J. Simon (ed.), *Pharmaceuticals for Developing Countries. Proceedings of an International Conference* (Washington, D.C.: Institute of Medi-

cine/National Academy of Sciences, 1979); "Pharmaceuticals and the Needs of Developing Countries," Institute of Medicine/National Academy of Sciences Policy Paper, Washington, D.C. 1979; Harold J. Simon, "Pharmaceuticals for Developing Countries: Interface of Science, Technology, and Public Policy," *Pharos* 44:9 (Spring 1981).

9. Agarwal, "Drugs and the Third World."

10. "Major Issues," UNCTAD, p. 60.

11. *Technology Policies in the Pharmaceutical Sector in Cuba* (Geneva: UNCTAD, 1980).

12. Simon, "Pharmaceuticals for Developing Countries."

13. Ibid., p. 63.

14. HEW Task Force on Prescription Drugs, *Final Report,* p. xiii.

15. Ibid., p. xii.

16. Agarwal, p. 17.

17. Ibid.

18. *The Selection of Essential Drugs. Report of a WHO Expert Committee.* WHO Technical Report Series 615 (Geneva: World Health.Organization, 1977).

19. Cited in Agarwal, p. 23.

20. Statement by International Federation of Pharmaceutical Manufacturers Associations, UNIDO Conference, Vienna, June 30–July 1, 1977.

21. Max Tiefenbacher (IFPMA), cited in Agarwal, p. 24.

22. Agarwal, p. 35.

23. Antonio Ruas, cited in Joseph Hanlon, "Are 300 Drugs Enough?" *New Scientist* 79:708 (September 7, 1978).

24. Agarwal.

25. Aida LeRoy (Health Information Designs, Washington, D.C.), personal communications, 1980, 1981.

26. G. Upunda, J. Yudkin, and G. Brown, *Therapeutic Guidelines. A Manual to Assist in the Rational Purchase and Prescription of Drugs* (Nairobi, Kenya: African Medical and Research Foundation, 1980).

27. Christopher Wood (AMREF), personal communication, 1980.

28. Agarwal, p. 30.

29. Ibid., p. 31.

30. Ibid., p. 30.

31. Ibid., p. 32.

32. *Pills, Profits and Politics,* pp. 140–143.

33. David Jones (Ciba-Geigy, Summit, New Jersey), personal communication, 1981.

34. *The Drugging of the Americas;* Milton Silverman, statement in U.S. Senate, Select Committee on Small Business, Subcommittee on Monopoly, *Pre-*

sent Status of Competition in the Pharmaceutical Industry 32:15360 (May 26, 1976); Philip R. Lee, ibid., p. 15377.

35. Albert Bowers (Syntex Laboratories, Palo Alto, California), personal communication, 1981.

36. Charles Medawar (Social Audit), statement before 10th World Congress, International Organization of Consumers Unions, The Hague, Netherlands, June 23, 1981.

37. Walter von Wartburg in "Pesticides and Pills: For Export Only," Public Broadcasting System television broadcast, October 7, 1981.

38. Charles Medawar, in statement cited above.

INDEX

Designer: Rick Chafian
Compositor: TriStar Graphics

Text: 10.5/14 Baskerville
Display: Optima

www.ingramcontent.com/pod-product-compliance
Lightning Source LLC
Chambersburg PA
CBHW031134270326
41929CB00011B/1620